BETWEEN THE TACKLES

Encouraging and Challenging Messages about Football and Faith

Tom Houck

Quote By
Dr. Lee Corder
NFL CHAPLAIN

BETWEEN THE TACKLES

Encouraging and Challenging Messages About Football and Faith

"A great book for football fans who want to put their faith into action"
— Dr. Lee Corder, NFL Chaplain

Tom Houck

Belleville, Ontario, Canada

BETWEEN THE TACKLES
Copyright © 2007, Tom Houck

All Rights Reserved. No part of this publication may be reproduced, stored in a retrieval system or transmitted in any form or by any means—electronic, mechanical, photocopy, recording or any other—except for brief quotations in printed reviews, without the prior permission of the author.

All Scripture quotations, unless otherwise specified are taken from the HOLY BIBLE, NEW INTERNATIONAL VERSION ®. Copyright © 1973, 1978, 1984 by International Bible Society. Used by permission of Zondervan Publishing House. All rights reserved. • Scripture quoataions marked NRSV are from the *New Revised Standard Version* of the Bible, copyright 1989, by the Division of Christian Education of the National Council of the Churches of Christ in the United States of America, and are used by permission. All rights reserved.

Library and Archives Canada Cataloguing in Publication

Houck, Tom, 1962-
    Between the tackles / Tom Houck.

Includes bibliographical references and indexes.
ISBN 978-1-55452-199-9

    1. Bible--Criticism, interpretation, etc. 2. Football--Religious aspects--Christianity. 3. Football--Miscellanea. I. Title.

BV4596.F6H69 2007   242   C2007-904916-8

**For more information or
to order additional copies, please contact:**

Tom Houck
www.faith360.org

Guardian Books is an imprint of *Essence Publishing,* a Christian Book Publisher dedicated to furthering the work of Christ through the written word. For more information, contact:
20 Hanna Court, Belleville, Ontario, Canada K8P 5J2
Phone: 1-800-238-6376 • Fax: (613) 962-3055
E-mail: info@essence-publishing.com
Web site: www.essence-publishing.com

To my awesome wife, Kimmie,

And my two favorite football players,

Matthew and Andrew

ACKNOWLEDGMENTS

I want to give special thanks to Dr. Lee Corder for his support and encouragement throughout this project. Lee is a chaplain for the Washington Redskins and is employed full-time at Young Life International. Despite a very busy schedule, Lee has been tremendously helpful and supportive. I am very grateful for this!

Thanks also to Brian Kush, a friend and passionate football fan who knows more about the sport than just about anybody I know. When I asked Brian to look at the manuscript, he responded by providing detailed comments and questions on every chapter. And he felt bad that he couldn't spend more time on the text!

Finally, I want to acknowledge my mother who has always been my biggest fan. I also want to thank my wonderful wife, Kim, who has fully supported my career change from business into ministry. She is also a great mother, and I am blessed to have such an awesome wife. Kimmie, I love you!

CONTENTS

Prologue: Are You Ready? 11
1. Clueless Fans 17
2. Giant Egos 23
3. A Player's Coach 27
4. Retaliation 33
5. Growing Pains 39
6. "My Bad, My Bad" 45
7. Making the Final Roster 49
8. Double Coverage 55
9. Going Over the Middle 61
10. There's a Flag on the Play 67
11. Playing in the Right System 73
12. A Lopsided Trade 79
13. Draft Day Busts 83
14. Taking Losses Too Hard 89
15. Wireless Speakers 95

16.	The Bottom of the Pile	101
17.	A Former Player	107
18.	Learning the Playbook	113
19.	Vocal Fans, Quiet Believers	119
20.	Moving the Chains	125

Epilogue: Leaving It All on the Field 131
Appendix: Forming a Discussion Group 135
Endnotes 139
Index of Biblical References 143
Index of Football Players, Coaches and Commentators 151
Index of Football Teams 155

PROLOGUE

ARE YOU READY?

Corinth was a sports town. Every two years, the Isthmian Games were held just outside of the prosperous city. In ancient times, this major sporting event ranked only behind the Olympics in terms of prestige and importance, attracting athletes and delegates from throughout the Greek-speaking world.

When the apostle Paul founded the church at Corinth, he lived there for 18 months. We don't know if Paul attended sporting events, but he was certainly aware of the Corinthians' interest in the Games. When writing to the church a few years later, he used an athletic analogy to make one of his most crucial points. In 1 Corinthians 9:24, he writes, "Do you not know that in a race all the runners run, but only one gets the prize? Run in such a way as to get the prize."

This wasn't the only time Paul utilized sports imagery. Nor was he the only religious leader to use secular illustrations to make theological points. Jesus often told parables about farming, money, family and mundane matters. The Lord knew his audience would better understand and retain the message if he spoke in the language of the people.

In today's culture, Americans love football. Without question, the sport has overtaken baseball as our national pastime. From the blistering heat of late summer to the dead of winter, millions of fans attend youth, college and professional games. Countless others watch gridiron action on television, participate in fantasy football leagues and compete in office polls. A plethora of radio and television shows, web sites, newspapers and magazines allow enthusiasts to monitor their favorite teams and players. The NFL Network even broadcasts 24 hours a day, seven days a week.

Americans also enjoy playing this game for entertainment. In our backyards. In flag football leagues. On video screens. Incredibly, first week sales of Madden '07 exceeded $100 million![1] Even the classic board game, Electric Football (remember the buzzing sound), has enjoyed a resurgence in the past decade.[2]

Thanks to the Internet, ESPN, NFL Network and other resources, football has become a year-round passion for a growing number of fans. These folks follow the NFL Draft, watch Scouting Combine performances, monitor free agent activity, and scrutinize roster and position battles during training camp. And that's just for the NFL!

I'm one of these fans. Since my childhood, I've cheered for my alma mater, the Penn State Nittany Lions. But my biggest passion is the New Orleans Saints. I never miss a game and regularly follow the team throughout the year. I live in Virginia, so I'm very thankful for the Internet and DIRECTV's "NFL Sunday Package."

Throughout my life, I've always considered football as an enjoyable hobby. But while completing graduate courses in seminary, I discovered a surprising benefit to my interest in the sport. I found myself using football analogies to explain

ARE YOU READY?

Biblical concepts. In class after class, professors and fellow students would hear me say, "It's like in football when...." Eventually, I figured I could write an entire book of devotionals. Yet I wondered if combining football and faith was appropriate. Was it perhaps irreverent or even cheesy? Then I remembered the traditions of Jesus and Paul and realized this makes perfect sense!

HOW TO USE THIS BOOK

This book features 20 chapters that explore important and practical aspects of the Christian faith. Why twenty? In the NFL, each team plays a minimum of 20 games per season: four pre-season contests and 16 regular-season games. You can read one chapter each week throughout the season, starting with your favorite team's first pre-season outing (you'll even get a bye week!). Alternatively, begin when the regular season starts and continue through the Super Bowl.

Of course, you can read this book as quickly as you'd like. You may also prefer reading during the off-season, especially if you struggle with "football withdrawal" when the season ends. Whatever your approach, I encourage you to reflect on the "extras" included at the end of each chapter. These include:

Personal Journal. Use this space to jot down key ideas or thoughts you want to remember. At the end of the book, I'll encourage you to revisit these pages and determine if follow-up is necessary.

Important Verses. These Biblical passages relate to the weekly topic. Consider memorizing verses that strike a chord. Memorization of Scripture is an excellent way to imprint God's Word on your mind and heart.

Extra "Film" Study. Great football players typically work harder than their opponents. Superstars like Peyton Manning and Ray

Lewis are well-known for putting in long hours in the film room. By identifying the subtle tendencies of their opponents, they gain an edge during games. With this is mind, I include extra Biblical readings that reinforce or expand on each chapter's theme. Additional study questions and exercises can be found at www.faith360.org.

Football Trivia. In several chapters, I include interesting statistics or trivia related to some part of the message. There is not any theological significance to this information—it's merely included because you are a football fan!

Keys to the Game

Early in most football telecasts, the broadcasting crew identifies "keys to the game" or "keys to victory." Examples include:
- Win the turnover battle;
- Keep Vince Young in the pocket;
- Score touchdowns (not field goals) in the red zone;
- Slow down Michigan's pass rush.

The "keys" usually sound simple, but a lot goes into making them a reality. Take the last example. To slow down a ferocious pass rush, the offense must rethink its blocking schemes. Tight ends or running backs may need to "stay in" and protect the quarterback. The offense might want to utilize more quick passes, play action fakes, draw plays, and even shuffle passes. Of course, players must execute their assignments and effectively make adjustments during the game.

While success hinges on the implementation of a myriad of details, the identification of broad goals is important. Overall objectives help players and coaches remember the critical success factors likely to influence the outcome of the game.

In our Christian journeys, Jesus provides similar "keys to the game." Let's pretend that ESPN's Suzy Kolber has obtained an on-the-field interview with Jesus before a pivotal game. "Coach," she asks, "What have you stressed to your team?" Unlike Broadway Joe Namath, Jesus focuses on the question. Ha, ha.[3] "Well Suzy," He explains, "there are two things. First, love God with all your heart, soul and mind. And the second is like it: Love your neighbor as yourself. If we do these things, Suzy, we'll be in good shape."

Of course, this image is silly; but the message is not. This was how Jesus responded when questioned by a Pharisee in Matthew 22:36-40. These two great commandments summarize the Holy Scriptures and provide overarching goals for all believers.

At the same time, we need additional guidance. Implementation of these principles isn't always easy or clear-cut, especially in today's complex world. In this book, we will explore these commands in a variety of contemporary situations.

Well, it's time to get started. The football is on the tee. The referee has given the go-ahead signal. The crowd is on its feet. Are you ready for some Faith *and* Football?

WEEK 1

CLUELESS FANS

You're no longer relaxing on the couch, eating munchies and sipping a soda. You are anxiously pacing in front of the television set, hoping the defense can hang on and preserve the victory. The announcer's voice fills the room: "It's third and four with 34 seconds to go...Carson Palmer lines up under center...He takes the snap...He's got plenty of time...Chad Johnson is open down the left sideline...It's a perfect throw, touchdown, Bengals!"

Ughhhhhh! For the second time in the game, Palmer connected with his star receiver for a big score. "Number 24 is terrible, I can cover better than him!" you utter in disgust, oblivious to your bulging waistline. It doesn't help your mood when the network shows a slow-motion replay of Johnson's creative end zone celebration.

Let's switch to a different scenario. Your favorite team has trailed all day but finally has an excellent chance to take the lead. The quarterback drops back and decisively throws a bullet...right into the arms of a linebacker. Interception! Game over. "What was he looking at?!"

Sound familiar? Just about every serious football fan has made similar remarks. But there's an old saying, "Appearances can be misleading." It's true in football, too. The reality is fans often don't have a clue when issuing harsh judgments against certain players or coaches. Their remarks are misguided.

Perhaps Chad Johnson was open because the cornerback, the infamous number 24, was expecting "over-the-top" help from the free safety that "bit hard" on a play-action fake. And maybe the quarterback who tossed the beautiful pass to a linebacker made a perfect throw. But the receiver ran the wrong pattern or broke off his route early.

This subject reminds me of Hannah and Eli. Not Eli Manning, but rather Eli the priest. In the first chapter of 1 Samuel (v. 10-16), Hannah desperately wants a child but is unable to conceive. While praying at the temple, tears stream down her face. Her eyes are bloodshot. Her lips move, but words don't come out. When Eli observes Hannah, he blurts out, "How long will you make a drunken spectacle of yourself? Put away your wine."

Oops! Eli jumped to the wrong conclusion about this decent woman. She wasn't drunk; she was in deep mourning. Eli's hasty remarks reveal the timeless relevance of another popular phrase, "Open mouth, insert foot."

Who hasn't made this kind of mistake before? Perhaps you've made unfair assumptions about a friend before knowing the facts. Maybe you arrived at unwarranted conclusions about a neighbor based on an isolated incident. Perhaps you allowed a stereotype to negatively taint your view of a business associate.

Last year, I visited a local water park with my oldest son. The facility included a great toddler's area for small kids. In the midst of happy and frolicking children, an angry woman stood out like a sore thumb. The scowl-faced lady repeatedly barked,

"Don't do that! Slow down!" at a cheerful girl playing harmlessly in the water.

Now admittedly, I'm somewhat paranoid with my young boy at the pool. But this woman went way overboard. "Lighten up!" I felt like screaming. Instead, I issued a cold glare in her direction. It was then, I realized, I was judging a person I knew nothing about. Perhaps this woman knew somebody who drowned or was severely injured in a water accident. Maybe her husband just left her, and frustration erupted at an inopportune time. Maybe the woman was indeed a nut! Even so, I wasn't in any position to cast judgment.

Luckily, the lady was too preoccupied to notice me. But when our judgments about other people become known, they are often hurtful or embarrassing. There is little good that can result from hasty conclusions or inaccurate impressions.

Even if we somehow possess the facts, the Bible warns against judging other people. Jesus said, "Do not judge, or you too will be judged…Why do you look at the speck of sawdust in your brother's eye and pay no attention to the plank in your own eye?" (Matthew 7:1,3). The apostle Paul added: "You, therefore, have no excuse, you who pass judgment on someone else, for at whatever point you judge the other, you are condemning yourself, because you who pass judgment do the same things" (Romans 2:1-2).

If you struggle with this temptation, remember that each of us is wired differently. We have different personalities, upbringings, influences, etc. that affect who we are. Consequently, we don't always face the same temptations or share identical weaknesses. Just because something is easy for me doesn't mean it's that way for you. In fact, you might be making remarkable progress although it doesn't seem like it by my standards.

In his classic book *Mere Christianity*, C.S. Lewis wrote,

"To judge the management of a factory, you must consider not only the output but the plant. Considering the plant at Factory A, it may be a wonder that it turns out anything at all; considering the first-class outfit at Factory B its output, though high, may be a great deal lower than it ought to be." 4

Only God can accurately make these judgments. Maybe that's another reason why He tells us not to try. Yet this sin tends to blossom as Christians become more knowledgeable about their faith. If you don't know what's in the Bible, you're less likely to harbor negative feelings towards people disobeying God's Word.

But when you *do* know, it's much easier to criticize and condemn those who ignore, ridicule, abuse or even struggle with God's standards. It's more tempting to judge them. Make derogatory comments. Feel disgusted or outraged. Or act in a patronizing manner. No wonder Christian author and educator Josh Hunt wrote, "In many cases, the world perceives us as being more judgmental, critical, and condemning." 5

Let's be frank. None of us are close to perfect. We all fall dramatically short of God's holy standards, and none of us are qualified to condemn or judge other people. What would you think of an offensive lineman who repeatedly commits "false starts" but angrily condemns a teammate penalized for holding? What if a receiver plagued with the "drops" criticizes another wide-out for struggling to get open on his routes? Shouldn't these players concentrate on their own deficiencies before worrying about other folks?

In the same vein, let's focus on our own behavior and conduct. Allow the Lord to judge His own servants. Not only is God the only One with all of the facts, He doesn't need help in doing His work!

Personal Journal

Write down any key points you want to remember:

_____

_____

_____

_____

_____

Important Verses

"Who are you to judge someone else's servant? To his own master he stands or falls...Therefore, let us stop passing judgment on one another" (Romans 14:4,13a).

"Man looks at the outward appearance, but the LORD looks at the heart" (1 Samuel 16:7).

"Therefore encourage one another and build each other up" (1 Thessalonians 5:11).

Extra "Film" Study

1. Read Luke 18:9-14. What can we learn from this parable?

2. Read John 8:1-11. What is the main point of this lesson?

WEEK 2

GIANT EGOS

Terrell Owens is a talented wide receiver possessing a rare combination of speed, size and strength. But in the middle of the 2005 season, the Philadelphia Eagles decided "enough is enough." The franchise suspended the attention-grabbing, disruptive receiver in mid-season although the team could have desperately benefited from his skills.

Despite this embarrassing episode, "T.O." quickly resumed his antics after signing with the Dallas Cowboys in the 2006 season. From training camp on, it seemed like Owens somehow managed to consistently make the headlines (mostly for non-football issues). Even while riding a stationary bicycle with a hamstring injury, Owens kept attention on himself by dressing up like Lance Armstrong. Yes, he even wore a cyclist's helmet!

Hall of Fame quarterback Steve Young played with the controversial star in the 1990s. He remembers Owens as a quiet and humble man. No, that's not a misprint. The wide receiver was regarded as a "shy country boy" when he joined the San Francisco 49ers in 1996. So, what in the world happened?

BETWEEN THE TACKLES

In a single word: success. In 1998, Owens enjoyed a terrific season, scoring 14 touchdowns and amassing nearly 1,100 yards receiving. When veteran superstars like Young and Jerry Rice left the 49ers, T.O. claimed the stage for himself and seized the limelight.

In a game against the Cowboys in 2000, Owens sprinted to the 50-yard line after scoring a touchdown and disrespected the Dallas "star." Both fans and players were offended by his actions. Subsequent scoring celebrations became increasingly creative and humorous; but his evolving behavior suggested deeper issues. Terrell Owens had become obsessed with "T.O." and being the center of attention. It was only a matter of time until he started disrespecting other players and coaches. Who can forget the images of Owens yelling at his Offensive Coordinator in San Francisco or verbally attacking Eagles' QB Donovan McNabb?

The T.O. saga reminds me of Saul, the first king of Israel. He started his reign as a humble man, but the "king thing" eventually went to his head. First, he considered himself above the law by disregarding established rules for offering sacrifices (1 Samuel 13:7-14). He then deliberately disobeyed God on the battlefield before building a monument to honor himself (1 Samuel 15). I wonder if Saul kept a Sharpie under his armor!

Human nature never changes. Famous athletes, entertainers and other bigwigs have always been susceptible to feelings of arrogance and self-importance. With legions of fans and commentators singing their praises (dare I even say "worshipping" them), it's easy to see how humility can melt like an ice cube in the Arizona heat.

Ironically, celebrities and high-profile individuals aren't the only ones with swollen heads. Even "ordinary" people with modest success are susceptible to big egos. Business executives.

Professors. Youth coaches. Store owners. Why, I bet you know some people who fit this bill. These folks believe they are very important. Their egos need to be stroked frequently. They fail to treat others with courtesy, empathy and respect. They always seek to be the center of attention.

In contrast, the most influential person in history went out of his way to teach and demonstrate humility—Jesus Christ. Indeed, the Bible is filled with exhortations to be humble. Not only does this include acknowledging our dependence on God, but respecting other people. The two concepts go hand in hand. If we fail to acknowledge an awesome Creator who cares about all of humanity, it's much easier to build up ourselves and look down on other people.

With this in mind, why do you suppose God picked Abram to be the father of his "chosen people?" He was a 75-year old man without children in a culture consumed with family lineage. Abram (later called Abraham) was a "nobody." He had no reason to be proud or boastful. But, the Lord told Abram, "I will make you into a great nation and I will bless you; I will make your name great" (Genesis 12:2).

Interestingly, Abraham's calling is found immediately after the Tower of Babel story in Genesis 11:1-9. This account describes ambitious men who wanted to "make a name" for themselves without acknowledging God. They wanted all the glory. And, yes, they failed. Meanwhile, Abraham remains a giant figure in Christianity, Judaism and even Islam.

In our culture, success is viewed as extremely desirable. But it doesn't come without perils. Proverbs 27:21 notes, a "man is tested by the praise he receives." If you're fortunate enough to taste the sweetness of success—any kind of success—be on guard against feelings of self-importance and arrogance. Your talents are God-given. And the Lord cares about every single person you encounter. Pray that your words and actions will please God and draw others to Christ. After all, He is the one who should be worshipped and glorified—not you or me!

Personal Journal

Write down any key points you want to remember:

_____
_____
_____
_____
_____

Important Verses

"For everyone who exalts himself will be humbled, and he who humbles himself will be exalted" (Luke 14:11).

"In humility consider others better than yourselves" (Philippians 2:3).

"Show proper respect to everyone" (1 Peter 2:17).

"You save the humble but bring low those whose eyes are haughty" (Psalm 18:27).

Extra "Film" Study

1. Read John 13:1-17. How does this message apply to your life?

2. Read Acts 14:8-18. Did Paul and Barnabas fail to take advantage of a great opportunity? What can you learn from their response to the crowd?

WEEK 3
A PLAYER'S COACH

Bill Cowher, head coach of the 2005 Super Bowl champion Pittsburgh Steelers, demanded excellence and held players accountable. When members of his team made dumb mistakes, he let them know it. Perhaps you remember the images of Cowher grabbing a player's jersey and yelling in his face. The passionate coach invoked fear in the hearts of many players.

At the same time, Cowher was widely known as a "player's coach" who genuinely cared about his players. He was often seen on the sidelines conversing and joking with members of the team. He earned the reputation of a loyal, caring and fair leader who built a special bond with his players. In return, they gave their best efforts to please and impress him.

No wonder Bill Cowher was the longest-active coach in the National Football League before stepping down in 2006. He found the right balance between discipline and compassion. Toughness and compassion. Love and fear.

Consider the alternatives. Nice or "soft" coaches tend to quickly lose control of a team. In the late 1990s, many onlookers believed Norv Turner suffered from this problem when serving as head coach in Washington. Conversely, tough coaches who manage ruthlessly typically find fear isn't an effective long-term motivator. Some folks put Tom Coughlin, coach of the New York Giants, in this category.

While a coaching analogy isn't perfect, I believe these concepts are helpful in attempting to understand our Creator. Let's begin by examining a key verse in the Bible. Deuteronomy 6:5 states, "Love the LORD your God with all your heart and with all your soul and with all your strength." Jesus declared that this was the greatest commandment in the Hebrew Scriptures.

A few verses later, Deuteronomy 6:13 presents a seemingly contradictory commandment: "Fear the LORD your God." William L. Holladay writes that the phrase "fear of God" often "conjures up for us visions of dour Puritans and sermons of hell-fire, which many of us have consigned to the dustbin of history." [6] Consequently, many folks today prefer focusing on God's love, mercy and compassion. We would rather think of Jesus holding little children and performing miracles. We recite Psalms that emphasize God's endless love. The image of the "Good Shepherd" brings us comfort and peace.

But while these depictions of Christ are accurate, do they represent the whole picture? The command to "fear God"—along with the phrase "the wrath of God"—are repeated hundreds of times throughout the Old and New Testaments. Surely we can't ignore such a major theme in the Bible. Maybe we should explore what "fear" really means.

The term has a variety of definitions and can arise from many sources. If a wild grizzly bear charges at you in the woods, you're likely to experience fear. Or pretend you are a quarterback playing against the Baltimore Ravens. While barking the signals behind an inexperienced offensive line, you notice linebacker

Ray Lewis is threatening to blitz. Uh-oh! Looking into Ray's steely eyes will probably create fear in your heart. In the bear example, you fear for your life. In the football example, well, you fear for your life!

A different kind of fear occurs when encountering an overwhelming power or force. Imagine standing close to the launch site when the space shuttle takes off or being in the midst of a powerful force of nature like a hurricane. It's natural to feel Small. Helpless. Vulnerable.

I believe the ancient Israelites experienced this type of fear when encountering God at Mount Sinai. According to Exodus 20:18-20,

> "When the people saw the thunder and lightning and heard the trumpet and saw the mountain in smoke, they trembled with fear. They stayed at a distance and said to Moses, 'Speak to us yourself and we will listen. But do not have God speak to us or we will die.' Moses said to the people, 'Do not be afraid. God has come to test you, so that the fear of God will be with you to keep you from sinning.'"

Read Moses' words carefully. The great leader states, "Do not be afraid" just before mentioning the "fear of God." How interesting. He's suggesting we can fear God without being frightened. No wonder many scholars contend the phrase "fear God" should be interpreted as being filled with reverence and awe.

Let's try a short exercise. Try to imagine the power necessary to create our amazing universe or earth. Imagine the force needed to create and sustain life, perform miracles, control the weather and more. Oh, I realize such power is unfathomable, but try anyway. If you have any imagination, perhaps this exercise provides a tiny glimpse into God's omnipotence.

Now, imagine yourself standing in God's presence. No wonder the Israelites were scared. No wonder Isaiah cried out, "Woe to me! I am ruined!" (Isaiah 6:5). Even Moses was "afraid" and "hid his face" at the burning bush (Exodus 3:6). Why? The Creator of the universe was speaking directly to him. How awesome!

Put another way, God's power and gloriousness is intimidating, even overwhelming. It's critical that we never lose this image of God. If we only focus on His love, mercy and forgiveness, it's easy to ignore God's call for holiness and obedient living. If we think only of Jesus' kindness and compassion, it's easy to fall victim to "cheap grace." That's when we don't take sin seriously. After all, Jesus loves us and will forgive us. Like the football team that doesn't respect the coaching staff and fails to perform at maximum capacity, we fail to reach our potential as human beings.

On the other hand, if we only view God as wrathful and judgmental, it's difficult to love the Lord with all our heart, mind and soul. We might not like God at all. Any attempt to walk as a faithful disciple is unlikely to last long.

So, balance is the key. One of my favorite Biblical passages is the story of the Transfiguration when Jesus took three disciples on a mountain for an encounter with God (Matthew 17:1-8). At that moment, God made an important announcement: "This is my Son, whom I love; with him I am well pleased. Listen to him!" The disciples "fell facedown to the ground, terrified." They had experienced God's awesome presence and were given an imposing command.

But Jesus immediately placed his hands on them and said, "Get up...don't be afraid." When they raised their heads, they saw the face of Jesus. Without hesitation, Christ displayed love and concern for the frightened men.

Friends, I don't believe we can truly and fully love God until we appreciate His power, majesty, holiness and distaste for sin. It's these characteristics that make His love for us so thoroughly amazing. When we grasp this concept, it becomes even easier to love our great and awesome God. What a perfect Head Coach we have!

PERSONAL JOURNAL

Write down any key points you want to remember:

_____
_____
_____
_____
_____

IMPORTANT VERSES

"For as high as the heavens are above the earth, so great is his love for those who fear him" (Psalm 103:11).

"The fear of the LORD is the beginning of knowledge" (Proverbs 1:7).

"He tends his flock like a shepherd: He gathers the lambs in his arms and carries them close to his heart; he gently leads those that have young" (Isaiah 40:11).

BETWEEN THE TACKLES

Extra "Film" Study

1. Read the following accounts of humans who experienced God's presence: Exodus 19:16-19, Matthew 17:1-8, Isaiah 6:1-5 and Ezekiel 1:25-28. If you experienced such an encounter, how would you feel? Would this affect your everyday life?

2. Read Job 38-39. Does this passage help you to appreciate God's mighty power?

Football Trivia

Jeff Fischer of the Tennessee Titans is widely regarded as a "player's coach." With the departure of Bill Cowher from the Pittsburgh Steelers, Fischer became the longest-active head coach in the NFL. In 2007, he began his 14th season as the Titans' head coach.

WEEK 4

RETALIATION

It's so predictable. A football player pushes his opponent after the whistle blows. Maybe he throws a punch. Spits. Makes a derogatory comment about his manhood…or his mama. The opposing player decides to "get even" and responds in kind.

A yellow flag soars through the air. But the penalty isn't called on the original offender; the officials missed his transgression. The infraction is called against the player who retaliated, and the consequences are costly. A 15-yard "unsportsmanlike conduct" penalty. Ouch!

Not surprisingly, some players attempt to bait an opponent into committing this foul. You know, get under his skin. Tick him off. Send him over the edge. What an easy way to pick up 15 yards, right? In his book, *Next Man Up*, John Feinstein writes about Orlando Brown, a veteran offensive tackle for the Baltimore Ravens:

> "Brown was one of those people who was a delight to be around 99 percent of the time…But when he lost his temper, it could get scary in a hurry…Players on the

other teams often tried to bait him into committing penalties, either through trash talking or unseen grabbing and pushing in the pile. His temper had cost the team in the Tennessee playoff game when Jevon Kearse had taunted him into committing a personal foul just prior to the Ravens' final punt of the game. That 15 yards had allowed the Titans to get just close enough for Gary Anderson to sneak his game-winning 46-yard field goal over the crossbar."[7]

In our Christian journeys, we won't find any shortages of rude, mean and insensitive people. On a moment's notice, they can prompt us to act in an ungodly manner. A condescending salesperson. An aggressive driver yelling obscenities out the window. A bully harassing your child. A boss humiliating you in front of colleagues. A loud-mouthed fan in the bleachers shouting derogatory comments about your kid. An offensive or obnoxious neighbor or relative.

Maybe these folks are baiting us, maybe they're not. Either way, it's tempting to respond in kind. You want to defend your honor. Show you're not a weakling. Get in the last word. But like the retaliating player charged with a penalty, we often end up as the losers. Why? We're not living like God wants us to live. The Lord wants us to love our neighbors, maintain self-control and avoid the temptation of striking back or gaining revenge.

A wonderful example of restraint is found in 2 Samuel 16. King David was traveling to a town called Bahurim. During the journey, a man named Shimei followed the entourage and "pelted David and all the king's officials with stones."

What a fool! David could have ordered this man's execution immediately. In fact, one official approached David, saying,

RETALIATION

"Why should this dead dog curse my lord the king? Let me go over and cut off his head." But David resisted the temptation and instructed his servants to "Leave him alone."

Imagine the reaction of the king's officials and troops. Perhaps they called David a wimp (out of earshot, of course). Maybe they were just befuddled. They surely complained for the remainder of the journey. After all, "David and his men continued along the road while Shimei was going along the hillside opposite him, cursing as he went and showering him with dirt. The king and all the people with him arrived at their destination exhausted" (2 Samuel 16:13-14a). It sure would have been more convenient to retaliate and eliminate the irritant.

David wasn't always so wise. Before assuming the throne, he was a fugitive on the run because King Saul wanted him dead. To survive in a nomadic state, David and his followers protected the flocks of wealthy livestock owners from thieves and wild animals. These landowners customarily paid a "gratuity" for protecting their interests.

One time, David's men protected the flocks of a wealthy man named Nabal (1 Samuel 25). But they soon discovered this guy was a jerk. Not only did he refuse to pay the gratuity, Nabal insulted the men. When David became aware of this news, he was furious. Enraged. Ready to teach this loser a lesson. He immediately set out to kill Nabal and all the males in his household.

Luckily, Nabal's wife heard what was happening. Abigail quickly gathered food and ran to intercept David. She showered him with respect and urged David to ignore her foolish husband. She appealed to reason, suggesting David would later regret his hot-blooded response. Her efforts were successful. To his credit, David listened and agreed with this courageous woman. He showed restraint. Nobody would be hurt.

Without question, you and I will encounter situations where it's tempting to respond in kind. It will be difficult to bite our tongues. Hard to walk away. But if we're lucky, an Abigail will be there to help maintain our composure. Just be sure to listen.

Better yet, pray the Lord will help you become increasingly like Jesus. Any fool can fight back, mouth off or retaliate. That's easy. But Christ chose the more difficult path of showing love, restraint and forgiveness—even when He was mistreated and falsely accused. This doesn't sound wimpy to me. It sounds like a "real" man of God.

Personal Journal

Write down any key points you want to remember:

_____
_____
_____
_____
_____

Important Verses

"A gentle answer turns away wrath, but a harsh word stirs up anger" (Proverbs 15:1).

"A fool shows his annoyance at once, but a prudent man overlooks an insult" (Proverbs 12:16).

"Make sure that nobody pays back wrong for wrong, but always try to be kind to each other and to everyone else" (1 Thessalonians 5:15).

RETALIATION

"Do not repay evil with evil or insult with insult, but with blessing, because to this you were called so that you may inherit a blessing" (1 Peter 3:9).

EXTRA "FILM" STUDY

1. Read Judges 15. What does this passage reveal about the cycle of revenge?

2. Read Galatians 5:22-23 and Colossians 3:12-15. Are these traits consistent with a person who seeks retaliation?

WEEK 5

GROWING PAINS

The speed of the game is dramatically faster. Defensive schemes are more complex. Playbooks are gigantic. Media scrutiny is intense. The season is longer. The pressure, especially if a lucrative contract was signed, can be overwhelming.

Welcome to the NFL. It's no wonder a rookie quarterback struggles when adjusting to the new level of competition. Rarely does he resemble the all-star who delighted crowds at his alma mater. The once-confident athlete now makes uncharacteristic mistakes. Holding the ball too long in the pocket. Making the wrong reads. Taking too long in the huddle. Throwing inaccurate passes. Fumbling snaps. Staring down receivers.

It's even more frustrating when the young quarterback repeatedly makes the same blunders. After all, he "knows better." Discouragement can easily settle in. Self-confidence can disappear.

Fortunately, these rough times rarely last forever. The game eventually "slows down" as the quarterback gains experience.

Nevertheless, the long-term prognosis doesn't seem to bring much consolation for the athlete going through the transition. The days can be long and difficult.

Consider Peyton Manning, star quarterback for the Indianapolis Colts. In 1998, he suffered through a difficult rookie season, throwing more interceptions than touchdown passes. In the subsequent season, his performance improved considerably. Peyton's completion percentage jumped from 56.7 to 62.1 percent while throwing 26 touchdown passes versus just 15 interceptions. He was voted into the Pro-Bowl and has been one of the league's premier quarterbacks ever since. In 2004, he broke Dan Marino's record by tossing 49 touchdown passes.

Manning's transition period was fairly brief according to NFL standards. Many coaches believe it takes a quarterback three years to grow into a consistent and effective player. Successful players such as Vinny Testaverde and Rich Gannon took even longer to mature and develop.

Do you ever feel like a rookie quarterback in your Christian journey? I'm not referring to the length of time you've been a believer, but rather how you're practicing your faith. Maybe you're not living the way you want to live. You make the same mistakes over and over, even after promising they won't happen again. Perhaps it's losing your temper. Criticizing your spouse. Drinking too much. Lacking patience with an elderly parent. Engaging in inappropriate sexual thoughts or activities. Yelling at your kids. Whatever.

You may feel rotten, guilty or hopeless. Deep down, you wish your behavior was different. You would love to snap your fingers and instantly change. You would love to be like those folks who seemingly have no flaws. Instead, you find yourself saying, "Ahhhh, why did I do that again?" "I know better, but I just can't seem to help myself." "What's wrong with me? Why can't I change?"

Is this frustrating? You bet! But like the young quarterback experiencing growing pains, we must not be consumed with feelings of discouragement or defeat. We need to adopt a broader, long-term perspective. The reality is that spiritual growth and maturity come slowly for most people. Despite our best intentions, most of us find ourselves committing undesirable actions or entertaining unhealthy thoughts. Even the apostle Paul wrote, "I do not understand my actions. For I do not do what I want, but I do the very thing I hate." (Romans 7:15 NRSV) It doesn't matter how long we've been a believer or how far we've progressed. None of us are close to achieving perfection.

Fortunately, our wonderful God is so incredibly patient. Even when we mature at a snail's pace—no, even when we backslide—the Lord never abandons or gives up on us.

So we don't need to be stressed out, guilt-ridden or defeated. That's not what God wants for us. Jesus conquered sin on the cross (Hebrews 9:28). The Lord forgives our sins when we repent (1 John 1:9) and wants us to experience joyful and abundant lives (John 10:10).

Please don't misunderstand. I'm not encouraging anybody to be content with weaknesses or sinful tendencies. Indeed, one of the biggest problems in Christianity today is that so many believers are complacent about obedience. It's important to take our shortcomings seriously.

Just don't beat yourself up in unhealthy ways. As C.S. Lewis wrote, "The main thing we learn from a serious attempt to practice Christian virtues is that we fail."[8] How true! Fortunately, God provides a remedy through Jesus Christ and will help transform us into better persons. It just doesn't always happen instantaneously.

So, let's give praise and thanks to our wonderful God for His infinite love, mercy and patience. Ask the Lord for the power and strength to head in the right direction. Oh, it may take longer than we'd like to change deeply ingrained behaviors. But like Jesus said, "With God all things are possible" (Matthew 19:26).

The Lord is your biggest fan. He wants to help you succeed.

Personal Journal

Write down any key points you want to remember:

_____
_____
_____
_____
_____

Important Verses

"Here is a trustworthy saying that deserves full acceptance: Christ Jesus came into the world to save sinners—of whom I am the worst" (1 Timothy 1:15).

"If you love me, you will obey what I command" (John 14:15).

"I can do everything through him who gives me strength" (Philippians 4:13).

"For I am convinced that neither death nor life, neither angels nor demons, neither the present nor the future, nor any powers, neither height nor depth, nor anything else in all creation, will be able to separate us from the love of God that is in Christ Jesus our Lord" (Romans 8:38-39).

Extra "Film" Study

1. Read 1 Timothy 1:12-17. Reflect on God's patience during your lifetime.

2. Read 1 Corinthians 13:4-8. Since God is love (see 1 John 4:8), how does this passage make you feel?

Football Trivia

In 2007, 43-year old Vinny Testaverde was signed by the New England Patriots. After a horrendous start in the NFL, who would have predicted that Testaverde would have been playing two decades later? In 1987, the University of Miami star debuted as quarterback of the Tampa Bay Buccaneers. It wasn't pretty. In 1988, he threw 35 interceptions. It wasn't until 1993 when his touchdown passes exceeded the interceptions. He continued to improve with age, enjoying excellent seasons with the Ravens, Browns and Jets. Today, Testaverde ranks 6th and 9th in all-time passing yards and touchdown passes, respectively.

WEEK 6
"MY BAD, MY BAD"

Football is a complex sport, causing players to frequently make mental mistakes. Occasionally, fans observe a guilty player pointing at himself on the field, indicating, "My bad, my bad." This, of course, means, "It's my fault. I messed up."

Some players are, however, reluctant to accept responsibility for their blunders. They are more likely to point the finger of blame in a different direction. At a teammate. An official. The media. The hotdog man. Okay, not the hotdog man, but just about anyone else. A few years ago, quarterback Aaron Brooks even blamed the fans in New Orleans for his poor performance on the gridiron.

In our lives, we face similar temptations. There will be times when we are caught doing something stupid or flat-out wrong. But rather than admitting our mistakes, we find it tempting to place the blame elsewhere. "If it wasn't for that person or thing, I would have never done it," we rationalize. Maybe we're embarrassed. Perhaps we're stubborn or scared. Whatever the reason, many of us are quick to offer denials, deflections and excuses for our behavior.

Finger pointing has been around a long, long time. When God approached Adam and Eve about eating from the forbidden tree, Adam quickly blamed Eve. She then blamed the serpent. Adam even told God, "The woman you put here with me—she gave me some fruit from the tree" (Genesis 3:12). The woman *you* put here! It sounds like Adam implied that God was responsible for his sin.

Another classic example was depicted in the classic movie, *The Ten Commandments*, starring Charlton Heston. Near the end of the film, Moses climbed Mount Sinai to meet God while his brother Aaron remained in charge of the people. When Moses didn't return promptly, the crowd became impatient and Aaron led the infamous effort to build a golden calf.

Of course, Moses eventually returned and couldn't believe what had happened. Despite Aaron's obvious role in this disgraceful act, he denied any wrongdoing. Aaron pleaded with Moses, "Do not be angry…they gave me the gold, and I threw it into the fire, and out came this calf!" (Exodus 32:1-24).

Out came the calf! I mean, it just magically appeared, dude. This was like saying, "I don't know how your CDs ended up in my stereo cabinet" or "I have no idea why these fictitious expenses appeared on my expense report" or "I don't know how a woman's panties ended up in my suitcase." Out came the calf! Can you say, *lame?*

One of the things I love about the Bible is that it doesn't sugarcoat reality. The Holy Scriptures are filled with examples showing us how *not* to act in the world. The Bible so accurately portrays human nature and the sinfulness of human beings.

At the same time, the Bible provides many positive examples. When King David committed adultery with a woman named Bathsheba, he could have easily blamed other people (2 Samuel

"MY BAD, MY BAD"

11:2-5). Why, it was Bathsheba's fault for bathing in a spot where David could see her naked body. It was her husband's fault for going off to war and leaving a beautiful woman alone. It was his wives' fault (yes, David had more than one) for not adequately satisfying his physical needs. Why, it was even God's fault for giving David a strong sex drive.

But David, a powerful king who could get whatever he wanted, didn't offer these half-baked excuses. When the prophet Nathan confronted him about his transgression, David immediately acknowledged his mistake. He didn't make excuses or blame anyone else. In 2 Samuel 12:13, he readily admits, "I have sinned against the LORD." Compare this to Cain's denial in Genesis 4. The murderer denies any knowledge of his crime by uttering the famous line, "Am I my brother's keeper?" (Genesis 4:9).

Psalm 51 is widely thought to be a prayer of confession in which a repentant David asks for forgiveness. He writes, "Against you, you only, have I sinned and done what is evil in your sight…Create in me a pure heart, O God, and renew a steadfast spirit within me." The king was contrite and truly sorry.

I once heard a pastor describe the Christian journey this way: "It's not that committed Christians don't sin," he explained, "because we do. Even though we seek to avoid sin, we face temptations like everyone else. But when we mess up (which we will), we humbly confess, try to make things right, and attempt to change our ways."

When our actions adversely affect other people, ask God and the offended persons for forgiveness. Right away. Go the extra mile and make things right. Denials and cover-ups usually make matters worse. They may even make us look silly. Just like Adam and Aaron.

BETWEEN THE TACKLES

Personal Journal

Write down any key points you want to remember:

_____

_____

_____

_____

_____

Important Verses

"If we claim to be without sin, we deceive ourselves and the truth is not in us. If we confess our sins, he is faithful and just and will forgive us our sins and purify us from all unrighteousness" (1 John 1:8-9).

"You are forgiving and good, O Lord, abounding in love to all who call to you" (Psalm 86:5).

Extra "Film" Study

Read Geneses 4:1-10 and Psalm 51. Compare the responses of Cain and David after committing horrible sins.

WEEK 7
MAKING THE FINAL ROSTER

Each summer, a perennial ritual begins as training camps open across the country. Aspiring athletes battle heat, humidity, fatigue, injuries and other challenges with the hopes of making a team's roster.

What are the chances for success? Let's do the math. An NFL team invites more than 80 players to training camp. Only 53 make the final roster while another eight players are named to the developmental "practice squad." This means the dreams of roughly two dozen men are dashed when receiving the notice to pack their bags.

Perhaps these discarded players lack the necessary speed, size or strength to play in the NFL. Maybe they struggled to learn the playbook. Perhaps they weren't able to contribute on *special teams*, a key factor for players on the bubble. Maybe an untimely injury forced them to spend too much time in the training room. Whatever the reason, these players missed their opportunity to impress. They failed to perform and were shown the door.

A lot of folks think an individual's eternal fate is also impacted by performance. Billy Graham remarked,

"I've been preaching for more than fifty years...I always say the same thing. Yet you ask the common man on the street what I say is the way to heaven, and nine of ten will say, you need to live a good life, follow the Golden Rule, make positive choices, go to church, be nice to people, and do the right things." [9]

If you're a good person, such thinking goes, your reward is eternal life in a glorious place called heaven. If you're a bad person, well, let's just say your destination isn't so pleasant. This sounds fair and simple, but an unsettling question is unavoidable. How do we know if we're "good" enough? Are we "good" because we've never been convicted of a serious crime? Are we "good" because we're better than our next-door neighbor or the unscrupulous jerk at work? Seriously, how does God keep score?

Some believe angels keep track of our deeds. If positive deeds outweigh the negatives, an individual receives a ticket to paradise. I can picture the scene now. Every Monday, the angels sit in a dark room watching film. Grading every move you make, every thought in your head. Their goal? To arrive at a score to add to your lifelong tally.

Even if true, this knowledge doesn't do us any good because we still don't know our score! We don't know if our roster spot is secure or if we're about to be cut. Should we try extra hard to impress the angels, or can we "play it safe" and simply avoid major mistakes?

Let's be frank. If admittance to heaven is based on performance, knowing where we stand (and how much time remains) is critical. Yet the scoreboard is blank. God doesn't reveal this information. Nor can we keep score ourselves like kids playing football in the backyard. We don't know how much credit to give for specific deeds, positive or negative. Surely, they can't be equally weighted. Suppose a child molester helps an old lady cross the street, are his deeds offset? What if a bank robber drops ten bucks in the offering plate, is it a wash? What if he gives $100? How about $10,000?

I'm sure you understand my point. This is a silly and impossible endeavor to undertake. Except for a few saints, I presume—maybe Mother Teresa, Martin Luther King Jr. or Pope John Paul II—most folks won't have any assurances about heaven. Don't you find this idea troubling? How you deal with a loved one's death or your own mortality? How does a person experiencing extreme hardship have hope?

Fortunately, our loving God doesn't leave us in the dark. The Lord doesn't want us to guess, worry or despair. Ephesians 2:8 proclaims: "For it is by grace you have been saved, through faith—and this not from yourselves, it is the gift of God—not by works, so that no one can boast." In Galatians 2:16, Paul makes the same point: We "know that a man is not justified by observing the law, but by faith in Jesus Christ."

Do you see anything in these verses about good deeds or performance? Salvation comes from belief and faith in Jesus Christ. God has shown incredible mercy and love by making it easy for us to acquire eternal life. Our scores don't matter. We can confidently experience the joy and hope the apostle Paul repeatedly writes about in his letters (e.g., 1 Corinthians 2:9).

It almost sounds too good to be true. No wonder it's hard for many humans to accept. How can a "bad" person go to heaven? It's not fair. Terrible individuals deserve to "rot in hell." Have you heard that before? Have *you* said that before?

Fortunately, we're not in charge. We don't come close to matching God's mercy, love and forgiveness. And since the Bible declares that none of us meet God's holy standards, we can be thankful the Lord provides this awesome means of obtaining salvation.

As noted earlier, this doesn't mean we can live however we please. James 2:17 states that "Faith by itself, if it is not accompanied by action, is dead." In other words, *real* faith not only saves us, but it changes us. Oh, we're still far from perfect; but we become more like Christ. Our actions are the by-products or "fruit" of our faith. It's an important distinction.

What's the bottom line? The Lord wants us to love, obey and put our trust in Him. Famous Victorian author George MacDonald wrote, "God is easy to please, but hard to satisfy."[10] But unlike the coach who cuts players for not performing at a high level, God won't remove us from the roster when we mess up. He won't rescind the inheritance promised to His children.

When we truly grasp these concepts, it should make us passionate about serving and pleasing our awesome God. Obedience is no longer a burden or hassle. We'll want to bless the world by becoming a "better" person. We just don't have to worry about keeping score!

PERSONAL JOURNAL

Write down any key points you want to remember:

___

___

___

___

___

MAKING THE FINAL ROSTER

IMPORTANT VERSES

"For God so loved the world that he gave his one and only Son, that whoever believes in him shall not perish but have eternal life" (John 3:16).

"If you confess with your mouth, 'Jesus is Lord,' and believe in your heart that God raised him from the dead, you will be saved" (Romans 10:9).

"Believe in the Lord Jesus, and you will be saved" (Acts 16:31).

EXTRA "FILM" STUDY

Read Luke 23:39-43. What does this story suggest about eternal life?

WEEK 8
DOUBLE COVERAGE

The media loves scandal, controversy and bad news. It figures the viewing public would rather hear the tawdry details of the Minnesota Vikings' "love cruise" than uplifting stories about players in their communities. This is a shame since so many athletes are excellent role models making positive differences in the lives of others.

Take Warrick Dunn, star running back of the Atlanta Falcons. Dunn formed a successful foundation that helps single mothers purchase their own homes. As of 2007, Dunn's organization assisted 60 mothers and over 140 children in achieving their dream of home ownership.[11] He also challenged every NFL player to contribute five thousand dollars to rebuild homes after Hurricane Katrina devastated the Gulf Coast. His efforts raised nearly $2 million for this important cause.[12]

Then there's Reggie Bush. After the Heisman Trophy winner was drafted by the New Orleans Saints in 2006, he wasted no time in contributing to his new city. Before signing his first NFL contract, Bush pledged $86,000 to resurface a football field used by six local high schools and donated

$56,000 to keep open a financially troubled school serving special-needs children. Brian McCarthy, the NFL's director of corporate communications, commented, "Reggie Bush has redefined the team impact player. Everything points to him being an impact player on and off the field."[13] Local residents were so moved by his generosity they called him Saint Reginald after a 13th century saint.

I mention two high-profile players, but so many athletes raise or donate money to worthy causes. While I don't know the motivations of every generous individual, it's clear that much of the world's generosity is practiced by Christians putting their faith into action. Following the example of Jesus. Obeying teachings that permeate the Bible. For instance:

> "When you reap the harvest of your land, do not reap to the very edges of your field or gather the gleanings of your harvest. Do not go over your vineyard a second time or pick up the grapes that have fallen. Leave them for the poor and the alien" (Leviticus 19:9-10).

> "There will always be poor people in the land. Therefore I command you to be openhanded toward your brothers and toward the poor and needy in your land" (Deuteronomy 15:11).

> "If anyone has material possessions and sees his brother in need but has no pity on him, how can the love of God be in him? Dear children, let us not love with words or tongue but with actions and in truth" (1 John 3:17-18).

> "Command those who are rich in this present world not to be arrogant nor to put their hope in wealth, which is so uncertain, but to put their hope in God, who richly

provides us with everything for our enjoyment. Command them to do good, to be rich in good deeds, and to be generous and willing to share" (1 Timothy 6:17-18).

Despite the clarity of these verses, many of us battle two opponents when it comes to parting with our hard-earned possessions: selfishness and insecurity. The tandem is a formidable tag team, keeping us in "double coverage" at all times. Imagine a receiver trying to get open if Champ Bailey and John Lynch of the Denver Broncos are constantly covering him. It's a huge challenge.

Here's a personal example of how selfishness and insecurity work together. When I pick up my checkbook to tithe or contribute to a good cause, these opponents frequently rush to the scene. Insecurity begins the assault by whispering in my ear, "Have you forgotten about college tuition for your kids? It keeps rising, you know. What if your income declines? What if your family incurs unexpected medical bills? What if something major goes wrong in your house? How will you ever reach your retirement goals?"

"Okay, okay! Those are good points," I respond. "Maybe I should write the check for a smaller amount." That's mistake number one. Now the opponents smell blood. Selfishness enters the scene. "Tom, I thought you wanted a high-definition television to watch the games? How sweet would that be? And don't forget the new car you want. Seriously, aren't you embarrassed when it's your turn to drive colleagues to lunch? And, hey, let's not be selfish. Your wife really wants a remodeled kitchen. Doesn't she deserve the best? I thought you loved her...."

My resistance crumbles. "Well, I suppose my wife and I already give away more money than a lot of people," I reason. "How much of an impact will this cash make, anyway? Nobody will notice the difference." Game over. I've been defeated.

Do you struggle with insecurity or selfishness? If so, the Bible is one of the best tools to defeat these opponents. Do you remember when Jesus watched people make offerings at the temple (Mark 12:41-44)? The money poured in as "many rich people threw in large amounts." But Jesus was most impressed with a poor widow who only gave two copper coins. Why? She made a real sacrifice. On Earth, those coins didn't make much of a difference. But in heaven, the impact was huge. What an important lesson that directly addresses a common reason for clinging to our possessions.

The apostle Paul provides another inspiring example in 2 Corinthians 8. In verses 1-4, he praises God for the generous financial support supplied by the Macedonian churches. Even while living in poverty, these believers "gave us much as they were able, and even beyond their ability." Paul adds, "Entirely on their own, they urgently pleaded with us for the privilege of sharing in this service." Wow! The Macedonians didn't own much but considered it a "privilege" to help others. They acted "entirely on their own," not in response to pressurized fundraising campaigns, feelings of guilt or a desire to gain public recognition. Why? They felt "overflowing joy." King David and the ancient Israelites felt a similar joy when contributing assets to build a magnificent temple for God (see 1 Chronicles 29).

Let's be honest. Many of us spend our lives trying to earn and accumulate money. No wonder it's hard to give away. But if we love our fellow human beings, we'll gladly loosen the grip on our wallets. Instead of hoarding wealth or constantly splurging on ourselves, we'll be eager to advance God's kingdom on Earth. We will want to tithe and help other people.

PERSONAL JOURNAL

Write down any key points you want to remember:

_____
_____
_____
_____
_____

IMPORTANT VERSES

"A generous man will prosper; he who refreshes others will himself be refreshed" (Proverbs 11:25).

"Do not say to your neighbor, 'Come back later, I'll give it tomorrow'—when you now have it with you" (Proverbs 3:28).

"Each man should give what he has decided in his heart to give, not reluctantly or under compulsion, for God loves a cheerful giver" (2 Corinthians 9:7).

EXTRA "FILM" STUDY

1. Read Luke 12:13-34. How does this passage address selfishness and insecurity?

2. Read 1 Chronicles 29. What are the main themes in this chapter?

WEEK 9
GOING OVER THE MIDDLE

Hines Ward isn't afraid to go over the middle. The star receiver of the Pittsburgh Steelers makes tough catches in traffic, absorbing punishing hits from linebackers and defensive backs. Ward also loves to block on running plays. Such efforts aren't glamorous and usually don't appear on highlight reels, but the team player knows they can mean the difference between winning and losing.

A lot of receivers prefer to avoid such contact. They would rather run deep patterns or scamper out of bounds after making a catch. They are prone to "short-arming" the ball when attempting catches in heavy traffic. Rather than fully extending to make a reception, these guys prematurely pull in their arms to protect their bodies from incoming defenders (this is also referred to as "alligator arms"). The result is an incompletion or interception. Unlike Ward, these players are often labeled as "finesse" or "soft" receivers.

In the last chapter, we addressed the importance of making financial contributions to churches and other worthwhile causes. As Proverbs 3:9 plainly declares, "Honor the LORD with your wealth." At the same time, it's not enough to merely donate money to people in need. Do you think Jesus wrote checks from a desk while allowing other folks to provide hands-on assistance? No way. Jesus was on the front lines, willing to get His hands dirty. Longing to go over the middle.

When we begin loving people like Christ, we also want to go over the middle. Visit nursing homes and hospitals. Lend support and compassion to mourning families. Travel on mission trips. Feed the homeless. Help a friend or even a stranger deal with a personal crisis. Maybe it's job loss. Divorce. Infertility. Unwanted pregnancy. Miscarriage. Parenting struggles. Financial pressures. Aging. Death. Serious illness. There are just so many opportunities to go over the middle!

Unfortunately, our opponents from the last chapter—insecurity and selfishness—refuse to go away. Have you ever turned down opportunities to help others because you weren't sure you had the necessary skills to help? Have you ignored a sick or dying person because you didn't know what to say? Have you avoided certain topics with friends or acquaintances because the subject matter is uncomfortable? If the answer is "yes," insecurity has made you afraid to go over the middle.

Not long ago, I read a useful book entitled *Don't Sing Songs to a Heavy Heart: How to Relate to Those Who Are Suffering* by Dr. Kenneth Haugk.[14] This easy-to-read paperback offers practical advice on what to say and, just as importantly, what not to say to persons who are suffering. After finishing the book, I realized Christians are frequently encouraged to extend compassion but are given minimal, if any, practical guidance on how to do so effectively. This must change.

Perhaps this type of book can help in your efforts to serve those in need. Maybe you'll even want to receive more formal instruction. Many churches, for instance, offer training programs that enable individuals to become Stephen Ministers.[15] The program is excellent but requires a significant time commitment. Well, this leads to my next point....

In today's hectic and overscheduled world, too many believers lack the time to help other people. But, here's the big question. Isn't busyness often a form of selfishness? As followers of Christ, it's critical that we evaluate how we spend our time. Our life is a precious gift from God, isn't it?

I'm not suggesting that Christians abandon their careers, family and all recreational pursuits. These are important aspects of our lives. But at the same time, many folks have allowed these areas to command too high of a priority. Consequently, we lack the time to invest in other people and put our faith into action. In too many cases, there's "no give" in our schedules. No cushion.

You know, it's easy to rationalize and make excuses. This is when it's wise to hear some straight talk from Jesus. The parable of the sheep and the goats (Matthew 25:31-46) is blunt:

> "Then he [the Judge of the world] will say to those on his left, 'Depart from me, you who are cursed, into the eternal fire prepared for the devil and his angels. For I was hungry and you gave me nothing to eat, I was thirsty and you gave me nothing to drink, I was a stranger and you did not invite me in, I needed clothes and you did not clothe me, I was sick and in prison and you did not look after me.'"

The people quickly denied they did anything like that. "Not us, Lord," they responded. But Jesus replied, "I tell you the truth, whatever you did not do for one of the least of these, you did not do for me."

With Jesus' words fresh in your head, I wonder how pleased God is when we repeatedly use the excuse, "I'm too busy." My guess? Not very. If we are committed to pleasing God, we'll make time to help other people. Not out of obligation, but out of gratitude and love.

As we learn to love God's people, our heart will long for opportunities to reach out. Even more than contributing money, we'll find it's an absolute blessing and privilege to serve other human beings. Like Christ, we'll be eager to go over the middle.

PERSONAL JOURNAL

Write down any key points you want to remember:

_____
_____
_____
_____
_____

IMPORTANT VERSES

> "Let us not become weary in doing good, for at the proper time we will reap a harvest if we do not give up. Therefore, as we have opportunity, let us do good to all people" (Galatians 6:9-10).

> "Then Jesus said to his host, 'When you give a luncheon or dinner, do not invite your friends, your brothers or relatives, or your rich neighbors; if you do, they may invite you back and so you will be repaid. But when you give a banquet, invite the poor, the crippled, the lame, the blind, and you will be blessed. Although they cannot repay you, you will be repaid at the resurrection of the righteous" (Luke 14:12-14).

GOING OVER THE MIDDLE

Extra "Film" Study

Read Matthew 25:31-46.

Football Trivia

Each year, the Pacific Club IMPACT Foundation selects defensive players in college football who make the most impact on and off the field. The winner receives the Lott Trophy. For more information, visit www.mcspoll.com/lotttrophy.htm.

WEEK 10
THERE'S A FLAG ON THE PLAY

Imagine a football game with no rules. Anything goes. Linemen are allowed to hold. Defensive backs can tackle receivers before the ball is thrown. Quarterbacks can throw forward passes after crossing the line of scrimmage. Pass rushers can lead with their helmets!

Sounds crazy, huh? Without rules—and officials to enforce these rules—football would not be football. It would no longer resemble the sport we know and love. Pure chaos would result. Rules *must* be enforced to ensure a fair game.

Despite this reality, many fans loathe officials and their pesky yellow flags. Even when the "zebras" make the correct calls (which they usually do), it's tempting to blame them when transgressions are called against our favorite teams. As bearers of bad news, they are convenient scapegoats.

These thoughts popped into my head while working on a research paper at seminary. My assignment was to analyze a passage about the Mosaic Law in Romans 7. The apostle Paul's view on this important topic—the role of the law—has been studied and debated for centuries. As I wrestled with this challenging topic, I found my thoughts turning to the gridiron.

Let's back up for a moment. After Moses led the Israelites out of slavery in Egypt, the group encountered God at Mount Sinai. There God revealed the Ten Commandments and a host of laws covering ethical behavior, civic punishments and more. This body of regulations, found in the first books of the Bible, is often referred to as the Mosaic Law (or simply "the law").

In the New Testament, Paul writes frequently about this subject. Some folks have concluded that Paul was critical of the Mosaic Law. After all, one of his recurring themes is that the law brings death to all people. Paul declares "The wages of sin is death" (Romans 6:23) and "All have sinned and fall short of the glory of God" (Romans 3:23). In Galatians 3:10 (NRSV), Paul cites the Hebrew Scriptures: "Cursed is everyone who does not observe and obey all the things written in the book of the law."

Such statements are troubling for many believers. Why did God create imperfect people and expect them to adhere to laws they can never fully obey? And why is the punishment so severe? What was the Creator thinking? Was this a flawed plan that was ultimately corrected by Christ?

Let's think it through. Like a football game with no rules, a society without moral rules would quickly turn into complete chaos. It only makes sense the Creator of the universe would establish guidelines or rules to live by. Of course, the revelation of God's law at Mount Sinai went much further than merely introducing a few rules that people can follow with little difficulty. Instead, God revealed what holiness is really like, graciously revealing Himself through the law. He showed us what to strive for in our attitudes and conduct. God didn't "dumb down" the standards so everyone can easily comply.

For believers serious about serving and pleasing our Lord, this is a wonderful gift. If God had not revealed His standards, we would unknowingly live contrary to our Creator's wishes and be alienated from God. As Paul explains, "if it had not been for the law, I would not have known sin" (Romans 7:7 NRSV).

The Psalmist also describes this blessing in Psalm 19:7-8,10:

"The law of the LORD is perfect, reviving the soul. The statutes of the LORD are trustworthy, making wise the simple. The precepts of the LORD are right, giving joy to the heart. The commands of the LORD are radiant, giving light to the eyes…They are more precious than gold, than much pure gold; they are sweeter than honey, than honey from the comb."

Here's the big question. How do *you* view God's commands for holy living? Do you find them burdensome? You know, strict rules that prevent you from enjoying life. Or do you agree with the Psalmist? The reality is, while sin can be tempting and tantalizing, experience teaches us that following God's laws brings a plethora of benefits and blessings. Breaking the law is what often brings hardship and strife in our lives.

Nevertheless, we're stuck with the fact we're unable to comply with these laws. Yet ironically perhaps, this is also a benefit. An acknowledgment of our shortcomings is instrumental in developing humility. Let's face it, a lot of Christians are self-righteous and judgmental even when falling far short of God's holy standards. Can you imagine what they'd be like if God set the bar low and they actually achieved perfection?

Well, this possibility will never happen because the law is so demanding. We mess up a lot. It's important to recognize this is our own fault—not God's or the law's. In Romans 7:7 (NRSV), Paul rhetorically asks, "What then should we say? That the law is sin? By no means!" In other words, we are responsible for our actions. God did not create robots; He gave us a healthy dose of free will to make choices.

Once again, a football analogy helps us in understanding this concept. When a player commits pass interference or a personal foul, it's not the league's fault for writing the rule. It's not the official's fault for throwing the flag. It's the player's fault for committing the infraction!

"But," you might respond again, "God created us this way." This is true and leads to a key point. God knows we can't live perfect lives, and the "wages of sin is death." But God also offers a remedy. He offers the free gift of salvation "through faith in Jesus Christ to all who believe" (Romans 3:22). In other words, God wants us to humbly turn to Him for salvation and deliverance, something we can't achieve on our own.

God has always wanted humans—made in His image—to love, depend on and trust in Him. We were not created to ignore, neglect and rebel against our Creator. So, yes, we're imperfect; but God provides us with a Savior. It's a brilliant plan. Thanks be to God!

PERSONAL JOURNAL

Write down any key points you want to remember:

_____
_____
_____
_____

IMPORTANT VERSES

"So the law was put in charge to lead us to Christ that we might be justified by faith" (Galatians 3:24).

"I lift up my hands to your commands, which I love, and I meditate on your decrees" (Psalm 119:48).

"The entire law is summed up in a single command: 'Love your neighbor as yourself'" (Galatians 5:14).

EXTRA "FILM" STUDY

1. Read Psalm 119. Identify key verses that reveal the Psalmist's attitude toward God's laws.

2. Read Galatians 3. In your own words, attempt to explain the purpose of God's law, including how it should be applied today.

WEEK 11
PLAYING IN THE RIGHT SYSTEM

Goliath was a beast, a monster-of-a-man. Think Baltimore Ravens' offensive tackle, Jonathan Ogden (6'9", 345 pounds).[16] On this particular day, the Philistine warrior was engaged in some serious trash talking. "This day I defy the ranks of Israel!" he taunted. "Give me a man and let us fight each other" (1 Samuel 17:10).

None of the Israelite solders were willing to accept Goliath's challenge. But out of the blue, a little shepherd boy stunned everyone by announcing he would take on the intimidating giant. That's right, David, the little boy who played the harp. Think veteran kicker Martin Gramatica (5'8", 170 pounds).[16] Talk about a mismatch.

Despite laughter and ridicule from the Israelite soldiers, David convinced King Saul to allow him to fight Goliath. He then accomplished one of the biggest upsets in history by leveling the giant. The Israelites loved their new hero, and David was rewarded with lucrative endorsements from sneaker and soda companies. He even appeared on the cover of Madden 980 B.C. Hee, hee.

The battle of David and Goliath is well known, but there's an important part of the story many people don't know. After David convinced King Saul he could indeed defeat Goliath, the Bible states Saul "dressed David in his own tunic. He put a coat of armor on him and a bronze helmet on his head." But David responded, "I cannot go in these because I am not used to them." He removed the armor and looked for some stones (1 Samuel 17:38-40). The rest is history.

It's a good thing David spoke up when Saul saddled him with heavy, awkward-feeling equipment. It may have been easier to keep quiet. After all, this was the king's own equipment that he used in battle. It was an honor to be offered the royal gear. Nevertheless, it didn't feel right to David. It wasn't comfortable. It wasn't a good fit.

Not long ago, the New England Patriots won three of four Super Bowls, a remarkable accomplishment in the era of free agency. While other teams routinely paid big bucks for high-profile free agents or drafted the most gifted athletes, the Patriots built a powerhouse by acquiring players who fit their system. Intelligence, versatility and commitment to team were essential traits.

The importance of fitting in the right system can not be overemphasized. It allows players to thrive and maximize their abilities, increasing chances for success. In his book *The Blind Side*, Michael Lewis describes how Bill Walsh essentially invented the West Coast Offense in the 1980s to "compensate for the deficiencies of his quarterback."[17] Conversely, even talented players will fail to reach their potential if stuck in the wrong systems.

I believe this same idea applies to our spiritual journeys. First, it's important to our spiritual health to find a church where we can truly experience God in weekly worship. Researcher George Barna found that one-half of regular churchgoers failed to experience God's presence "at any time during the past year."[18] While this is tragic, it's not surprising. Just look around the congregation during most worship services. There is no shortage of individuals unenthusiastically mouthing the words of songs or struggling to pay attention during sermons. Many folks are bored, especially men. No wonder so many people have given up on attending church regularly.

What about you? If you attend church, do you regularly feel God's presence during worship? I mean, really feel it. You're certain the Living God is real and in your midst. There's no question about it. Maybe you experience a warm feeling or even goose bumps at times.

If you wonder what in the world I'm talking about, it may be time to rethink where you attend church. Unlike a few decades ago, there are many types of mainstream churches in 21st century America. Whether you prefer big or small, formal or casual, organs or guitars, long or short sermons, stained glass windows or modern auditoriums, there is probably a church for you. Unless you live in an area with limited options, you should be able to find a format that allows you to worship and connect with God. Sure, it may require courage to break out of your comfort zone and visit different churches, but this is a critical matter.

Now, I realize church isn't the only place to experience God. Many people feel close to their Creator in nature. Some when studying the Scriptures. Others in prayer or through the arts. If you connect with God in these ways, by all means, continue to do so! But the Scriptures emphasize the importance of communal worship with other believers. Finding a church home that "fits" should be on our priority lists.

In addition, it's important to realize that church membership should encompass more than weekly worship. It's essential that we study God's Word and participate in different ministries. Christians are not called to be isolationists. But again, don't be a square peg in a round hole. Find ways to learn and serve that are exhilarating and rewarding. If your church doesn't offer such opportunities, then again, maybe it's time to look around.

Like football players, we need the right system to thrive. If you're bored at church (or have abandoned weekly worship), you're probably in the wrong system. Ask God for guidance about this important matter. Experiencing God is powerful. Learning about God is fascinating. Serving Christ is rewarding. Living in Christian community is a blessing. When you operate in the right system, your faith will soar to new heights.

PERSONAL JOURNAL

Write down any key points you want to remember:

_____
_____
_____
_____
_____

IMPORTANT VERSE

"Draw near to God, and he will draw near to you" (James 4:8 NRSV).

EXTRA "FILM" STUDY

Read 1 Samuel 17

PLAYING IN THE RIGHT SYSTEM

FOOTBALL TRIVIA

Most football fans have heard of the "Madden Cover Curse." The theory is simple. After a player appears on the cover of EA Sports' wildly popular video game, he will be cursed with a serious injury or poor performance in the following season. Recent victims of the "curse" have included Marshall Faulk, Michael Vick, Donovan McNabb and Shaun Alexander.

WEEK 12
A LOPSIDED TRADE

In April 1999, football fans learned the terms of a blockbuster trade between the Washington Redskins and New Orleans Saints. And then they laughed.

Saints' coach Mike Ditka had fallen in love with a stud running back from the University of Texas named Ricky Williams. "Da Coach" wanted the Heisman Trophy winner and sure Hall of Famer at any cost. But Ditka's huge mistake was making his intentions known to the entire world, thereby losing any chance of negotiating a favorable deal. Not only was he forced to trade the Saints' entire draft class in 1999 to obtain the Dreadlocked One, but he gave Washington a first and third round pick in the 2000 draft. Talk about mortgaging one's future! This was one of the most lopsided trades in NFL history.

The Ricky Williams deal reminds me of an ancient story found in the first book of the Bible. In Genesis 25, we are introduced to the twin sons of Isaac: Esau and Jacob. The older son, Esau, lived for the moment. He didn't consider the long-term consequences of his actions. Esau wanted pleasure and gratification now. Sound familiar? After drafting Williams, Ditka noted, "We did the thing we thought would make us best, fastest." [19]

Back to the story. One day, Jacob was cooking stew when a famished Esau returned from a long day in the country. Esau was starving and could have eaten a horse. How sweet that dinner must have smelled. But rather than sharing the delicious meal with his hard-working brother, Jacob sensed an opportunity for personal gain. "Esau, first sell me your birthright." (Genesis 25:31)

Ah, the birthright. This was given to the firstborn male in the family and included a double portion of the father's estate, along with special authority and status in the family. It was highly prized, although the benefits were not received until the father died, similar to a modern-day inheritance. Knowing Esau's impulsive personality, Jacob made a lopsided proposal: dinner for birthright. Perhaps to Jacob's amazement—we don't know for sure—his foolish brother accepted the offer and devoured the meal. I hope it was tasty!

Over the years, many folks have called Jacob a thief for "stealing" his brother's birthright. But doesn't that seem like a bum rap? After all, they made a deal. It was an arm's length transaction between two consenting adults. Yet even so, was Jacob's behavior admirable? Was it appropriate to take advantage of his weak sibling? Would it have been more godly to protect his brother from such impulsiveness, rather than capitalizing for selfish gain?

Perhaps Jacob should have followed the example of his grandfather, Abraham. When a land dispute began brewing with his nephew, Abraham immediately took the high road and allowed Lot to pick the land he wanted. Abraham said, "Let's not have any quarreling between you and me, or between your herdsmen and mine…If you go to the left, I'll go to the right; if you go to the right, I'll go to the left" (Genesis 13:8-9). When

A LOPSIDED TRADE

considering Abraham was Lot's elder and the land on the right was far more desirable, this was an extremely generous offer. And Lot quickly snatched the best land for himself.

Poor Abraham had tried to be nice, but it seems like Lot took advantage of him. Maybe Abraham wasn't very bright. Perhaps he was just naïve. Or maybe, just maybe, Abraham was more interested in peace and harmony than personal gain.

Now, please don't misunderstand. I'm not suggesting the Redskins should have rejected the Saints' trade offer. This was a business transaction with both sides acting in what they believed were their best interests. I don't believe it's wrong for negotiators to seek favorable deals when conducting business. Free enterprise and the pursuit of self-interest are beneficial to society in many ways.

But where do we draw the line, especially in our personal lives? When does "driving a hard bargain" become "taking advantage of someone?" When does "looking out for oneself" result in trampling on others? Does it matter if you're dealing with friends or strangers? Does it matter if it's a personal or business setting?

These can be tough questions. My hunch is that most of us cross the line on occasion. Perhaps many times. It's human nature to look out for Number One. Quite frankly, we're more like Jacob than Abraham. The desire to please ourselves means we frequently ignore the concerns of others or even take advantage of them.

God calls us to act differently. To consider the interests of others before our own. To live in peace and harmony with fellow citizens. To forgive enemies and help the less fortunate. All of these commands are just different ways of saying, "Love your neighbor as yourself." Imagine what the world would be like if everyone did this.

BETWEEN THE TACKLES

PERSONAL JOURNAL

Write down any key points you want to remember:

_____

_____

_____

_____

_____

IMPORTANT VERSES

"Make every effort to live in peace with all men" (Hebrews 12:14).

"A good name is more desirable than great riches; to be esteemed is better than silver or gold" (Proverbs 22:1).

"If it is possible, as far as it depends on you, live at peace with everyone" (Romans 12:18).

EXTRA "FILM" STUDY

1. Read Genesis 25:29-34. What is your reaction to Jacob's deal with Esau?

2. Read Genesis 13:1-11. What is your reaction to the decisions made by Abraham and Lot?

FOOTBALL TRIVIA

The Saints selected Ricky Williams with the fifth pick in the 1999 draft after trading with the Redskins. New Orleans had previously made a similar trade proposal to the Cincinnati Bengals in hopes of acquiring the third overall pick in the draft. The Bengals rejected this offer and drafted quarterback Akili Smith.

WEEK 13
DRAFT DAY BUSTS

Ryan Leaf was an all-American quarterback and Heisman trophy finalist at Washington State University. In 1998, the San Diego Chargers selected him as the second overall pick in the NFL draft. Unfortunately for Chargers fans, Leaf became one of the biggest busts in draft history. *Wikipedia* notes "his time as a pro was short and marked by failure, which according to critics was largely due to his immaturity, arrogance, and poor work ethic." [20]

Leaf isn't the only player to squander his once-in-a-lifetime opportunity. In 2003, wide receiver Charles Rogers was also the second overall pick in the draft. But after making just 36 catches in his first three seasons, the Detroit Lions cut Rogers. One commentator attributed his lack of success to a poor work ethic, bad attitude and other problems.

Underachiever. Slacker. Flop. Bust. These words are often used to describe talented athletes who fail to reach their potential. Granted, it's not always a fair rap. Some players are simply overrated and don't have the ability to succeed at the next level. Others are plagued by unlucky or recurring injuries. But too many times, gifted athletes make poor decisions and throw away promising careers. They arrive at training camp out of shape or overweight. They take drugs or excessively drink alcohol. They aren't dependable, regularly showing up late for meetings and landing in the coaches' "doghouse." They might even lose the burning desire to succeed after receiving a big signing bonus. Whatever the reason, fans struggle to understand how such fortunate men can waste the opportunities so many kids dream about. Don't they realize how lucky they are?

Perhaps we should look in the mirror. It's often said Christians belong to "God's team." 1 Peter 2:9 proclaims, "You are a chosen people, a royal priesthood, a holy nation, a people belonging to God." What's our assignment? To love God and neighbor. To obey and serve the Lord. To advance Christ's kingdom on earth. All the stuff we've discussed in this book. But regrettably, many of us don't come close to fulfilling our potential—and we can't blame the outcome on injuries or lack of ability! Is it possible the descriptive words listed earlier apply to me and you? Slacker. Underachiever. Bust.

In Matthew 25:14-30, Jesus tells the parable of the talents. Even if you're familiar with this well-known story, it's worth reading again. Let's summarize by stating that God gives every person talents and abilities and it's important to develop and use them as part of our service to the Lord. Maybe it's leading Bible studies or volunteering at food banks. Perhaps it's participating in mission trips or serving elderly folks. Maybe it's working the audio booth at church or advancing God's kingdom in countless other ways. What a waste and shame when talented individuals choose not to use their God-given gifts in such ways. Instead, they focus on making money, seeking fame or simply enjoying themselves.

I'm not suggesting that all believers should become full-time pastors, youth directors, missionaries, social workers, etc. While these efforts are wonderful and essential, other occupations also provide vitally important ministry opportunities. In the secular workplace, Christians have the opportunity to interact with people who never read the Bible or attend church. They deal with individuals who hold negative stereotypes about believers. They routinely work with "nominal Christians" who believe in God but aren't serious about following Christ. What a tremendous opportunity for a committed believer to influence the world!

Now, what does this have to do with developing talents? It's simple. Colossians 3:23-24 states, "Whatever you do, work at it with all your heart, as working for the Lord, not for men, since you know that you will receive an inheritance from the Lord as a reward. It is the Lord Christ you are serving."

Martin Luther King Jr. put it this way:

> "If it falls to your lot to be a street sweeper, sweep streets like Michelangelo carved marble. Sweep streets as Shakespeare wrote stories. Sweep streets so well that all the hosts of heaven will have to say, 'Here lives the street sweeper who did his job well.'" [21]

In other words, be dependable and successful at work, regardless of your job.

I know what some folks are thinking. "Why would the Creator of the universe care about whether I hit my sales quota?" "Does God really care if I make a careless mistake when fulfilling an order?" "Why would Christ be concerned about my insignificant job with so many important things happening in the world?"

Mel Graham offers an explanation:

> "As Christians, we ought to do everything with vigor, dedication, commitment and excellence...When we demonstrate excellence, people will notice, and we will gain a platform for telling them about Jesus."[22]

Quite simply, our culture respects success. It is not impressed with losers or failures. When you perform well, people take notice. Customers. Colleagues. Suppliers. Hopefully, your boss, too! Such admiration and respect doesn't mean these folks will automatically be interested in your faith. But rest assured, if respect or admiration is absent, you'll have little chance of influencing them with words or actions.

In many occupations, increasing levels of success also expand one's circle of influence. You'll come into contact with more people. Washington Redskins' head coach Joe Gibbs has used football and NASCAR success to publicly proclaim his faith in Christ. Tony Dungy, the first African American coach to win a Super Bowl, describes his faith in the bestselling book, *Quiet Strength*. And how many people would have been interested in Arizona Cardinals' quarterback Kurt Warner's amazing faith journey if he had remained a stock boy at a grocery store in Canada?

Maybe you love your job, maybe you hate it. Perhaps you're excited about the future, maybe you're treading water. Either way, your performance at work or school (or even an extracurricular activity) matters to God. These are ministry opportunities. Make a commitment to perform to the best of your ability and excel in your chosen vocation. You'll have a stronger platform for sharing your faith and influencing other people.

At the same time, don't neglect ministries in the church or elsewhere that help other people or draw individuals closer to Christ. Churches and non-profit organizations always need volunteers. Always devote time for these crucial acts of service (see Week 9).

The choice is yours. You can become a perennial pro-bowler or a "draft-day bust"!

Personal Journal

Write down any key points you want to remember:

_____
_____
_____
_____
_____

Important Verses

"Whatever you do, whether in word or deed, do it all in the name of the Lord Jesus, giving thanks to God the Father through him" (Colossians 3:17).

"You are a letter from Christ…written not with ink but with the Spirit of the living God, not on tablets of stone but on tablets of human hearts" (2 Corinthians 3:3).

"We are therefore Christ's ambassadors, as though God were making his appeal through us" (2 Corinthians 5:20a).

"There are different kinds of gifts, but the same Spirit. There are different kinds of service, but the same Lord. There are different kinds of working, but the same God works all of them in all men" (1 Corinthians 12:4-6).

BETWEEN THE TACKLES

EXTRA "FILM" STUDY

1. Read Matthew 25:14-30. How does this passage apply to you?

2. Read Daniel 1. Does Daniel's example have relevance for your career?

FOOTBALL TRIVIA

From the web site, www.football.about.com, here are the top five "busts" in NFL draft history:

1. Ryan Leaf, QB, Washington State (2nd pick in 1998);
2. Tony Mandarich, OT, Michigan State (2nd pick in 1989);
3. Brian Bosworth, LB, Oklahoma (1987, 1st round of supplemental draft);
4. Akili Smith, QB, Oregon (3rd pick in 1999);
5. Lawrence Phillips, RB, Nebraska (6th pick in 1996).

WEEK 14
TAKING LOSSES TOO HARD

I never realized how much dust was in our sofa. After slamming my television remote into the cushion after yet another bogus penalty, I sat in amazement as the dust plume rose in the air, clearly visible in the afternoon sun.

I'm a guy who rarely loses my temper or becomes angry, but both were happening with increasing frequency on Sunday afternoons. Sometimes the catalyst was a careless turnover or a blown assignment resulting in a big play. More often than not, the impetus was an outrageous call by the officials. As the smirking zebra announced the infraction, I often found myself hurling the remote into the sofa as hard as I could. Overhand.

Before you jump to the wrong conclusions, let me offer a partial defense of my behavior. First, I never hurled the remote in front of other people. Neither did my frustration ever lead to cursing, breaking household objects, or smashing a hole in the drywall (as one of my friends once did).

Nonetheless, I wasn't proud. My wife could hear the thump of the remote in our kitchen, even with the stairway door closed. When she inquired about the strange noise coming from the basement, I played dumb. "What noise? You must be hearing things."

I'm not sure if she bought my response. But it became more difficult to hide my emotions if the Saints lost the game. "Why are you moping around?" she asked many times. "It's just a game." It sounded like she was trying to reason with my four-year-old son. "Why do you take it so personally?"

These were legitimate questions. It's not like I was friends with players or coaches on the Saints. Nor am I from Louisiana or anywhere else in the Gulf region. And, no, I don't bet on games. Yet for some odd reason, I found myself passionately consumed with the outcome of a contest between men I've never met. I know it sounds bizarre, but wait a minute, I bet some of you know what I'm talking about!

Well, one weekend during the 2005 season, I realized my childish behavior had to stop. Here's what happened. I was in danger of losing an important Fantasy Football game because my kicker was injured in the first quarter. Can you believe it? My kicker, for crying out loud! He pulled a hamstring and left the game after kicking just one extra point. I feared this unusual incident would cost me and later discovered my fears were justified. I lost my Fantasy match-up by one measly point that week.

In the meantime, the Saints were involved in a tight game. And then it happened. My boys in black and gold were robbed by the officials for the second straight week on a totally bogus call. You would think the zebras might give a team playing 16 road games just one break (this was the year of Hurricane Katrina), but *nooooo*. It seemed as if the officials were intentionally making calls against New Orleans to prove they weren't favoring the nomads. It was like when refs make two bad calls in a row against the same team so they can't be accused of "making things even." Do you ever think that happens? Sorry, I digress!

When the official announced this particular penalty, a dust plume exploded in my basement. As steam poured out of my head, my four-year-old son ran down the steps to greet me. "Hi Daddy!" he happily shouted. "Do you want to play with me?"

You can probably guess where this is headed. That's right, I snapped at him. Like *he* did something wrong. Do you remember *It's a Wonderful Life* when Jimmy Stewart lashed out at his daughter playing Christmas carols on the piano? It was kind of like that. But at least George Bailey had a decent excuse—his business and career were ruined. What was my reason?

Later that night, the words of Jesus inexplicably popped into my head. "If your right eye causes you to sin, gouge it out and throw it away…And if your right hand causes you to sin, cut it off and throw it away" (Matthew 5:29-30). Could the Lord actually be referring to football?

As the following weekend approached, I contemplated skipping my first Saints game in six years. It wouldn't be easy to do. My Sunday afternoon routine was an ingrained habit, and I felt as if I was betraying the team. Plus, I didn't like the idea of terminating—for no essential reason—such an impressive streak. I had watched 92 consecutive Saints games. It was kind of like Brett Favre's record of consecutive starts. Surely I could control my emotions better and keep the streak alive.

But the words of Jesus remained in my head. So on that particular Sunday, the television set remained off. I even unplugged my computer so I couldn't obtain real-time updates on my Fantasy Football team. It was going to be a football-free day. Not only did I survive, but I enjoyed a stress-free, pleasant afternoon with my wife and kids. I didn't feel like a reclusive loser in my basement for the first time in weeks!

Perhaps you struggle with tougher issues that need to be "cut out" from your life. Maybe your job causes fits of anger. Perhaps you're addicted to unwholesome entertainment. Maybe you hang out with bad influences. Perhaps your love of material pleasures limits your ability to tithe. Maybe you're a workaholic or golf addict or, yes, a hard-core football fan too busy to devote time to spiritual growth.

Be honest. What prevents you from living a godly life or growing in your faith? Pray about it. Ask your family and friends. If their responses are honest, you may discover it's time to rethink your priorities. God will be pleased.

My ban on football lasted just one week. The following Sunday, I resumed my normal routine without incident. Ever since, I've been determined to keep football games in perspective. I'll even play with my kids during the action (most of the time). But seriously, if I ever discover I'm slipping back into my old ways, I know what has to done. I'll have the scalpel ready.

PERSONAL JOURNAL

Write down any key points you want to remember:

_____
_____
_____
_____
_____

TAKING LOSSES TOO HARD

Important Verses

"Do not set foot on the path of the wicked or walk in the way of evil men. Avoid it, do not travel on it; turn from it and go on your way" (Proverbs 4:14-15).

"But when you are tempted, he will also provide a way out so that you can stand up under it" (1 Corinthians 10:13).

"Submit yourselves, then, to God. Resist the devil, and he will flee from you" (James 4:7).

Extra "Film" Study

Read Matthew 5:29-30. Do Jesus' comments apply to any aspects of your life? Are you prepared to take action?

Football Trivia

Do you know who caught Brett Favre's first pass in the NFL in 1996? It was Brett Favre! The pass was deflected and Favre made the reception.

WEEK 15
WIRELESS SPEAKERS

A few decades ago, quarterbacks called their own plays. As football became more complex, coaches took over this important duty. This approach offered many advantages but also consumed valuable time. First, the coach reviewed a voluminous listing of plays on his clipboard. After making a decision, he communicated the information to a player who ran onto the field. This man relayed the play to the quarterback who repeated the information for the players in the huddle. When the offensive unit finally reached the line of scrimmage, there wasn't much time to survey the defense, shift formations or call an audible.

In modern times, technology has streamlined this process. Coaches communicate directly with quarterbacks through wireless speakers in their helmets. Not only can coaches announce plays, they offer advice on managing the clock, strategy and more. With direct communication, misunderstandings are less likely to occur.

How awesome it would be if we could so easily hear from God. Maybe I'm mistaken, but it sure seemed easier to hear God's voice in the old days. Abraham conversed with God about the fate of Sodom and Gomorrah. Moses talked with God about many issues. Then there was Jacob. Joshua. Gideon. Samuel. Isaiah. Ezekiel. Job. The list goes on. And, oh yeah, let's not forget the countless people who heard the words of Jesus.

Does God speak to people today? Absolutely. Many persons have described hearing an actual voice, an audible sound. Probably more common is to experience some sort of feeling that God is instructing or calling one to action. Such communication is not verifiable by independent parties, but the person hearing God is usually certain about what the Lord communicated. Such experiences have led countless Christians to do wonderful things in the name of the Lord.

Unfortunately, there is another side to this story. Throughout history, human beings have also performed despicable acts after "hearing" from God. But did God really endorse the Crusades? Did the Lord command Christian leaders to execute people who disagreed with their complex theological positions? Does God encourage modern kids to strap explosives around their waists and blow up innocent civilians? Does the Lord instruct Christians to protest at funerals of homosexuals or slain American soldiers? Does the Holy Spirit tell a husband it's acceptable to cheat on his wife?

In many of these instances, I think individuals genuinely believe they are doing the will of God. They really "heard" the Lord's voice. But could they have been mistaken? Author John C. Maxwell observes that many Christ followers claim "God told me...." But Maxwell adds, "Over time, it often turns out that either God was wrong or that the person heard something other than God. Since God is never wrong...well, you get the picture." [23]

Perhaps the individual heard a more sinister force such as Paul describes in Ephesians 6:11-12:

"Put on the full armor of God so that you can take your stand against the devil's schemes. For our struggle is not against flesh and blood, but against the rulers, against the authorities, against the powers of this dark world and against the spiritual forces of evil in the heavenly realms."

On the other hand, maybe the "voice" isn't a spiritual force at all. Perhaps an individual's selfish desires are simply lodged in his head. Since "God loves us" and "wants the best for us," it's tempting to believe God will endorse any decision we make.

Now, I realize it's dangerous to question whether another person actually heard from God. None of us are in any position to make this judgment—unless God tells us what really happened (hee, hee). But seriously, the intent of this chapter is to examine our own lives. How do we know if we're truly hearing God? How can we improve the likelihood we're correct?

Here are a few observations. First, always pray and ask for God's help in discerning His will. This seems like a no-brainer, but it can be easy to forget. An associate of Billy Graham said a major difference between Graham and other leaders was that Billy would spend all night on his knees in prayer when a major challenged loomed.[24]

Second, it seems doubtful that God sends messages inconsistent with His nature. If our planned actions contradict the teachings of Jesus, do we really think God is speaking in our headset? The Didache, an early Christian worship manual from the first or second century, makes a similar point: "But not everyone who speaks in a spirit is a prophet, unless the person has the behavior of the Lord." [25]

This is a crucial point. It's one thing to accept a job because you think God is leading you in a new direction. Even if you're wrong, you're not committing a sin. Indeed, you can serve God in any employment situation. But it's quite another matter to commit violent or immoral acts after "hearing" from God.

Third, Maxwell notes "such communication is almost always reserved for unique and special—even singular—occasions. It is a huge deal to receive such communication from God and a huge deal to claim it." [26] I suppose Maxwell's theory is difficult to prove, and I'm sure a host of people will disagree. At the same time, I find it hard to believe that God concerns Himself with a lot of the trivial stuff that humans care about. But who knows?

Perhaps there's an obvious conclusion to grasp from this topic. Believers should display humility when attempting to discern God's will. David P. Gushee writes,

> "It might help us to remember that human beings (even Christian ones) are fallible...Surely there is plenty of biblical evidence of faithful people who misunderstood God's will or did not receive clear direction about every decision. Is it really impossible for us to say, 'I think I misunderstood what God was leading me to do'?" [27]

In contrast, some people are *soooo* confident about their frequent communications with the Almighty. Even if they are right, comments like "Yesterday, God told me to sign up for this aerobics class" rub many folks the wrong way. Indeed, some people feel inferior or frustrated when realizing that God doesn't communicate with them in such a manner. Loving Christians should never want to discourage fellow believers.

So, pray for guidance. Study the Scriptures. Be humble. And, yes, make sure your headset is turned on. The Lord may be trying to speak to you, but perhaps the crowd noise is too loud. This is, of course, an entirely different issue to address at another time!

Personal Journal

Write down any key points you want to remember:

_____

_____

_____

_____

_____

Important Verses

> "For my thoughts are not your thoughts, neither are your ways my ways" (Isaiah 55:8).

> "O my God, I cry out by day, but you do not answer" (Psalm 22:2a).

Extra "Film" Study

Read Genesis 15-16. What do you think of Abraham's decision to sleep with Hagar? Was he trying to follow God's will or simply doing things his own way?

Football Trivia

Did you know that a quarterback's wireless headset is automatically turned off when 15 seconds remain on the play clock? At that point, the quarterback can no longer hear the coach and is completely on his own.

WEEK 16
THE BOTTOM OF THE PILE

Football fans today have unprecedented access to players and coaches. With cameras and microphones on the field, in the locker room and on the sideline, nothing seems to escape our watchful eyes.

Unfortunately, there's one place cameras can't go. The bottom of the pile. We simply don't know what happens underneath the mass of men who converge on a loose football. The officials don't know, either, meaning it can get ugly. Anything goes. Biting. Pinching. Squeezing. Kicking. Poking. Twisting. You name it. No part of the body is safe.

In the 2006 season, Albert Haynesworth of the Tennessee Titans was suspended for five games after kicking and stomping on an opponent's face. On a national radio show, a star player from a different team was asked about the incident. He implied that nasty stuff routinely occurs at the bottom of the pile. Haynesworth's big mistake was committing his transgression in the open where he could get caught. If done under the pile, he explained, it's "part of the game."

This topic provides a rich analogy for our Christian lives. In public (oh, for example, let's say at church), people tend to act differently than at home or with close friends. One pastor used to laugh at the double standard. He often participated in golf outings with strangers who didn't know he was a Reverend. After lousy shots and missed putts, the men frequently uttered choice words. Eventually, somebody would ask, "So, what do you do for a living?" After revealing his vocation, the golfers turned beet red and quickly confessed that they "usually don't talk like that." Ha, ha!

Most of us realize the hypocrisy of two standards of behavior. Nevertheless, it is human nature to let our guards down with people we feel comfortable with or don't feel the need to impress. But consider this thought. When Jesus kicked off his sandals with the disciples after a long day, do you think he acted differently? Would Jesus diss folks he met earlier in the day, get intoxicated on wine or make lewd comments about Mary Magdalene's body? I don't think so!

Similarly, God wants us to seek holiness all of the time. 24/7. Regardless who we're hanging out with. The Bible states, "Just as he who called you is holy, so be holy in all you do" (1 Peter 1:15). This includes the thoughts and actions that nobody in the world, except you, knows about. The deep secrets of your heart.

Former U.S. Congressman and Oklahoma quarterback J.C. Watts Jr. has often said, "Character is doing the right thing when nobody's looking…There are too many people who think…the only thing that's wrong is to get caught."[28] In football, a similar comment is expressed: "It's only a penalty if you get caught." While this may be true in football, it's not the case in our personal lives. Proverbs 15:3 states, "The eyes of the LORD are everywhere, keeping watch on the wicked and the good."

THE BOTTOM OF THE PILE

Consider these excerpts from Psalm 139:1-4,

"O LORD, you have searched me and you know me. You know when I sit and when I rise; you perceive my thoughts from afar. You discern my going out and my lying down; you are familiar with all my ways. Before a word is on my tongue you know it completely, O LORD."

Some folks don't like it that God knows *everything*, even their dirtiest little secrets. But how would they feel if God took vacations during key moments in their lives? When they really needed Him.

Unlike an officiating crew, God always knows what is happening. And if we love the Lord, we will attempt to live in a holy manner that pleases Him. After all, sin is an affront to God. There's a great story in Genesis 39 describing how Joseph (yes, the guy with the multi-colored coat) refused to have an affair with the wife of his boss. Day after day, the beautiful woman made it clear she wanted "some action." Her husband was a busy man, so they surely could have gotten away with an illicit affair.

But Joseph resisted the temptation, even literally running away in one instance. He didn't want to betray the trust of his boss who had done so much for him. Even more importantly, Joseph did not want to "sin against God," who, by the way, had done even *more* for Joseph. Out of gratitude and love, Joseph didn't want to displease his Master.

Despite Joseph's example, many people commit "secret" sins if the risk of exposure by humans is minimal. But let's face it, there are no guarantees. Just ask Ted Haggard, the influential evangelical leader who was busted in October 2006 for allegedly using drugs and engaging in a homosexual affair.

When such secret sins are exposed, the damage is costly. Careers and families are ruined. Like a cornerback who plays well most of the game, the only thing history remembers is the player getting burned for the game-winning touchdown pass. One dumb mistake leaves a lasting impression.

What secrets are in your heart? Maybe your problem involves money. Perhaps you steal from an employer or lie to your spouse about spending. Maybe your challenge involves sexual temptation. Perhaps you despise certain people at work or are prone to holding grudges. Maybe you're insanely jealous of your sister. Perhaps you're secretly filled with anger. Did you know that the wife of the Pennsylvania man who murdered five Amish girls in 2006 apparently didn't have a clue about her husband's inner rage? The list of examples—both big and small—is endless. Isn't it amazing God still loves us, despite knowing everything in our hearts?

So, what's next? If it was easy to change our innermost thoughts and secret behaviors, we would have done so by now. But despite the potential consequences, many folks continue to play with fire. They can't seem to help themselves.

In such cases, there is only one thing to do. Repeatedly pray for divine assistance to overcome your problem. It might not happen quickly. In fact, a miraculous change may never happen (thank God we have a Savior!) But never underestimate the power of the Holy Spirit. Romans 8:11 says, "He who raised Christ from the dead will also give life to your mortal bodies through his Spirit, who lives in you." Wow! Think about this power. It has transformed the hearts and behavior of many, many people throughout history. So keep your head up. Try your best. Have faith. Nothing is impossible with God!

THE BOTTOM OF THE PILE

PERSONAL JOURNAL

Write down any key points you want to remember:

_____
_____
_____
_____
_____

IMPORTANT VERSES

"Nothing in all creation is hidden from God's sight. Everything is uncovered and laid bare before the eyes of him to whom we must give account" (Hebrews 4:13).

"I can do everything through him who gives me strength" (Philippians 4:13).

"No temptation has seized you except what is common to man. And God is faithful; he will not let you be tempted beyond what you can bear. But when you are tempted, he will also provide a way out so that you can stand up under it" (1 Corinthians 10:13).

EXTRA "FILM" STUDY

1. Read Psalm 139.

2. Read Luke 18:1-7. How frequently do you ask for God's divine assistance in overcoming temptation and sin?

WEEK 17
A FORMER PLAYER

Imagine you are a veteran wide receiver on a team with lofty expectations. In the off-season, your long-time Receivers Coach unexpectedly announces his retirement. A few weeks later, the phone rings at your home. The Head Coach wants your thoughts on filling the vacancy. "We have two finalists," he explains. "The first candidate is Jerry Rice."

How awesome! Jerry Rice is the greatest wide receiver in the history of the NFL. He was named to 13 consecutive pro-bowls and shattered the league's receiving records for receptions, yards, touchdowns and more.

"That's fantastic," you respond. "But, just out of curiosity, who is the other candidate?"

There's a pause before the coach awkwardly responds. "Uh, his name is Joe Thompson."

"Huh? Never heard of him," you reply. Another pause.

"Well," the coach explains, "that's because Joe never played or coached before. But he's the smartest guy I've ever met, and I think he can bring a lot of new ideas to our team. A fresh perspective, you know. I bet you'll learn a lot from him."

107

Hmmm. Joe Thompson may indeed be a smart guy, maybe the most intelligent human being since Albert Einstein. But would any sane person forego Jerry Rice? Not only is Rice a former player, but he played the position better than anybody else. Joe Thompson never caught a pass in his life! He never battled against the league's top defensive backs. He never struggled through injuries or the heat of training camp. He never had to hold his chin up after dropping consecutive passes. He was never taunted by opposing fans. Jerry Rice experienced all of these things and thrived throughout his career.

What's this have to do with faith? From the earliest pages of the Bible, God wanted a loving relationship with human beings. He continuously watched over the Israelites, performed wondrous miracles on their behalf, provided laws to improve their lives and led them to the promised land. Nonetheless, the people struggled to remember, honor and obey their Lord.

Now if I had been God, quite frankly, I would have given up on these disobedient characters. They were absolutely disgraceful. But instead, the Lord kept granting forgiveness and giving the Israelites more chances. And then He did something totally radical and amazing. A special baby was born to a virgin in Bethlehem. God decided to come in the flesh to redeem His people.

Oh, the Lord could have remained in the awesome splendor of heaven, never setting foot on Earth. He could have been content allowing multitudes of angels to worship at his feet. But not only did He come to Earth, the *way* He came and lived is even more remarkable. Why, Jesus could have arrived with great fanfare as the King of Kings. Imagine the Super Bowl half-time show the NFL's marketing team could have dreamed up! Jesus could descend from the sky amidst fireworks and flashing cameras. Then He could wow the crowd with miracles, including feeding the 80,000 people in the stadium—hotdogs and sodas for everyone!

After the game, Jesus could have insisted on royal treatment during His ministry. Staying at the finest hotels. Eating at the best restaurants. Hanging out with celebrities. Posing for photo ops with world leaders.

Of course, this sounds nothing like Jesus. As the fourth century theologian Athanasius wrote, "The Lord did not come to make a display. He came to heal and to teach suffering people."[29] Jesus entered the dirty trenches of this world to win our hearts. He hung out with disenfranchised and ordinary people. He participated in what common folks experience on a daily basis. Labor and rest. Joy and frustration. Happiness and sorrow. Good times and bad.

Because of these experiences, Jesus' teachings are extra real and credible. Yet many folks, especially followers of other religions, struggle to understand the Incarnation. One religious scholar writes, "It seemed logically impossible to claim (God) could be human. How could the omniscient, omnipotent and eternal creator and ruler of the universe become a human being?"[30] Well, uh, I'd reckon the scholar just answered his own question. God can do whatever He wants!

The author continues, "Could God have sunk so low as to have bowel movements, bad breath, and a runny nose? Even more shocking, could God really have been tempted to sin as a human being? Could he have suffered pain and died?"[31] Bruce L. Shelley puts such thoughts in context, writing that "Christianity is the only major religion to have as its central event the humiliation of God."[32]

That's the crux of the issue! Some folks refuse to believe God would stoop so low. The Lord is so great and magnificent that He is above such acts. He would never demean Himself in such a manner. But these people underestimate the extent of God's amazing love (Ephesians 3:18-19). God was willing to take extreme measures to save as many people as possible (2 Peter 3:9b). He wasn't prepared to sit by idly while people went astray and ruined their lives.

It's not that hard to understand. God created the entire universe, but He cares most about you and me. We are created in His image (Genesis 1:27). We are His potential heirs (Romans 8:17). If God is true love (1 John 4:8), it only makes sense that the Lord would takes these actions.

You've probably heard God sent Jesus to "save us from our sins." This is true. But I believe the real purpose of the Incarnation was broader. God wanted to give us a living, breathing example of how to love Him and treat other people. Sometimes a detailed instruction manual (i.e., the Mosaic Law) isn't enough; we need somebody to demonstrate. To show us how it's really done. Jesus accomplished this task perfectly.

Further, God wanted to demonstrate His incredible love for us. A love so strong the King of Kings was willing to join His subjects on Earth. To walk with us. Live like us. Serve us. Die for us. No wonder Jesus said, "No one has greater love than this, to lay down one's life for one's friends" (John 15:13 NRSV). In doing so, Jesus saved us from our sins and provided a means for eternal life.

Oh sure, God could have remained in heaven or demanded royal treatment on Earth. I suppose we would still be impressed. But more than anything, it was Christ's suffering, death and resurrection that have transformed the hearts of men, women and children for nearly 2,000 years. This is why so many people love and want to serve this "former player."

Personal Journal

Write down any key points you want to remember:

_____
_____
_____
_____
_____

Important Verses

"For you know the grace of our Lord Jesus Christ, that though he was rich, yet for your sakes he became poor, so that you through his poverty might become rich" (2 Corinthians 8:9).

"This is how we know what love is: Jesus Christ laid down his life for us" (1 John 3:16a).

"This is how God showed his love among us: He sent his one and only Son into the world so that we might live through him" (1 John 4:9).

"The LORD is gracious and compassionate, slow to anger and rich in love. The LORD is good to all; he has compassion on all he has made." Psalm 145:8-9

Extra "Film" Study

Read Isaiah 53. What does this passage tell you about God?

WEEK 18
LEARNING THE PLAYBOOK

I watched a NFL Films presentation showing Tampa Bay's Chris Simms (a rookie at the time) struggling to learn the complicated offense of Head Coach Jon Gruden. The young quarterback's head was spinning, and Gruden wasn't showing any mercy as he hurled complaints and insults at the young player. As a Saints fan, it's hard for me to have sympathy for a Buccaneer. But I actually felt sorry for the kid. Gruden was brutal!

Without a doubt, one of the major challenges when joining a new team is learning the playbook. It is a thick, intimidating document containing countless formations, plays and terminology. After Al Saunders was hired as the Washington Redskins' offensive coordinator in the 2006 season, it was widely reported that his playbook exceeded 700 pages!

While mastering a playbook may not seem like fun, it's absolutely essential. Regardless of a player's talent level, he won't see action on the field if he fails to know the plays. After all, one person's missed assignment can ruin an otherwise successful play.

Christians also have a playbook. Hall of Fame coach Joe Gibbs wrote, "Millions of people have come to the logical conclusion that the Bible is the best game plan for life that a person can ever discover. I hope you do, too."[33]

The Psalmist made a similar remark, "Your word is a lamp to my feet and a light for my path" (Psalm 119:105). Without question, the Bible's influence on human behavior and world history is unparalleled.

Ironically, most believers never read the entire Bible (or even significant portions). It's not that these individuals refuse to hold the Bible in high regard. They do. Most believe the Holy Scriptures are sacred and inspired from God. Further, the four Gospels (Matthew, Mark, Luke and John) are the only documents from antiquity that were canonized and describe the life, death, resurrection and teachings of Jesus Christ. But even so, a disturbingly large number of Christians aren't concerned about the dust gathering on the covers of their Bibles.

Why do so many Christians neglect the Holy Scriptures? Undoubtedly, the most popular reason is the Bible is frequently hard to understand. It's filled with hard-to-pronounce names, challenging teachings and ancient customs that are difficult to comprehend in today's world. Even Jesus' closest disciples were "in the dark." In Mark 4:13, Jesus notices the puzzled expressions on their faces and asks, "Don't you understand this parable?" In Mark 8:21, He inquires, "Do you still not understand?" In Matthew 15:12-16, it's actually sort of funny when Peter doesn't "get it." Jesus responds, "Are you still so dull?" For some reason, images of Jon Gruden (wearing his visor) pop into my mind!

Despite the complexity of the Bible, it's important to regularly study our playbook. It will help us be better prepared for the challenges we face on the field of life. Here are some quick tips that can make a big difference.

LEARNING THE PLAYBOOK

For starters, carefully choose the Bible translation that you read (yes, all English Bibles are translated!) Personally, I like the New International Version (NIV) or the New Revised Standard Version (NRSV). Others prefer even easier-to-read translations such as Eugene Patterson's *The Message*. If you own a King James Bible (the predominant translation used by past generations) and struggle with the language, take a trip to a bookstore and check out alternatives. People don't talk like that anymore!

Next, find resources to help you understand the text. At the minimum, acquire a "Study Bible" containing explanatory information in the footnotes or sidebars. You may also want to invest in *commentaries* that dive deeper into Biblical meaning. Your options are voluminous, ranging from scholarly works to plain-speaking books geared for beginners.

Finally, consider reading and studying the Scriptures with other believers. Maybe enroll in a class at church or join an organization such as Bible Study Fellowship, Community Bible Study, or others.[34] You can even form your own group with friends or participate in online forums. Just find a group where you feel comfortable and can truly learn.

Now, I have a confession to make. I was a Christian for nearly 30 years before reading the Bible from start to finish. But when it finally happened, the experience rocked my world. Of course, I can't promise your experience will match mine. As John Bunyan writes in his classic book, *Pilgrim's Progress*, "It is possible to learn all about the mysteries of the Bible and never be affected by it in one's soul."[35] Put another way, you can memorize the names of Israel's kings, recite pithy passages from Proverbs, and retell the stories of Jesus' miracles and parables—but never have your heart touched. Even John Wesley, founder of the Methodist movement, was a devoted Christian for years before he experienced a "strange warm feeling" that forever changed his life.

Similarly, a football player can memorize a playbook without "buying in" to the coaching philosophy or system. When this happens, it's likely to show on the field. Shortly before final cuts preceding the 2006 season, New Orleans' quarterback Drew Brees remarked, "I think the guys that are going to be left here come next week are going to be the guys who have bought into the system and believe in the things that coach has been teaching"[36]

Where do you stand in your faith journey? Are you passionate about Christ? Have you bought into your faith with heart, mind and soul? Do you feel in your bones that God loves and cares about you? Do you feel in your heart that you're placed on this planet for a reason? Are you filled with gratitude for what Christ has done in your life? Are you eager to serve on His team?

If your answers aren't yet a resounding "yes!" don't despair. James 4:8 promises, "Come near to God and he will come near to you." It might not happen immediately, but God keeps His promises. In the meantime, reading and studying the Holy Scriptures are great ways to learn about your Creator and His intentions for your life. It's a "must read" that may just rock your world.

Personal Journal

Write down any key points you want to remember:

_____
_____
_____
_____
_____

LEARNING THE PLAYBOOK

IMPORTANT VERSES

"Your word, O LORD, is eternal; it stands firm in the heavens" (Psalm 119:89).

"All Scripture is God-breathed and is useful for teaching, rebuking, correcting and training in righteousness, so that the man of God may be thoroughly equipped for every good work" (2 Timothy 3:16-17).

"For the word of God is living and active. Sharper than any double-edged sword, it penetrates even to dividing soul and spirit, joints and marrow; it judges the thoughts and attitudes of the heart" (Hebrews 4:12).

"These commandments that I give you today are to be upon your hearts. Impress them on your children. Talk about them when you sit at home and when you walk along the road, when you lie down and when you get up" (Deuteronomy 6:6-7).

EXTRA "FILM" STUDY

1. Read Mark 1:21-37. Despite a hectic schedule, how did Jesus find time to spend with His Father?

2. Read Luke 6:46-49. How can one put Jesus' words into practice unless he or she knows what they are?

WEEK 19
VOCAL FANS, QUIET BELIEVERS

Cheese heads in Green Bay. Dawgs in Cleveland. Scary-looking Raider fans in the Black Hole. Don't you enjoy watching obsessed fans in crazy outfits and costumes?

Of course, these are not the teams' only hard-core supporters. Countless fans purchase impressive supplies and merchandise. Clothes. Flags. Pennants. Inflatable chairs. Clocks. Pool balls. Bobbleheads. You name it. When these proud fans wear or display their purchases, they are making a public declaration about themselves. "I am a Seminoles fan!" "I am a Vikings fan!" "I love the Dolphins!" "I love the Trojans!"

Josh is one of these guys. He lives in the suburbs of Chicago and is employed as a mid-level manager at an insurance agency. Everyone knows he is a huge Bears fan. At home, he inflates a giant bear in his front yard on game day. At work, Josh's cubicle is adorned with Bears' paraphernalia, and he is recognized as the most knowledgeable fan in the office. He knows every player on the depth chart and can impressively recite obscure statistics and trivia.

Josh is also an outstanding person. He has an excellent reputation as a fair boss who treats everyone with dignity and respect. He always does "the right thing," and his calm responses to angry customers have inspired many co-workers. It is Josh's deep faith that motivates him to practice Christian values in the workplace.

There's just one problem. Nobody in the office knows Josh is a Christian. Not a single person knows Jesus Christ is the main reason for his goodness. His colleagues don't know he used to be jerk, mistreating employees at a previous employer. They aren't aware that he previously struggled with binge drinking and even cheated on his wife. They don't know anything about the God who made such a transformation possible.

Josh is what I call a "stealth" Christian. He keeps his faith to himself. Although he operates his life in an exemplary way, God receives none of the credit. This causes the words of Jesus to pop into my head: "If I glorify myself, my glory means nothing" (John 8:54).

Remember, Josh has no problem in expressing his devotion to the Bears. Just not Christ. Perhaps he wants to "fit in" with the younger non-believers in the office. Maybe he doesn't think such conversations are appropriate at work (although his neighbors don't know about his faith, either). Perhaps he is worried about the legal ramifications of speaking openly. Maybe he just feels uncomfortable talking about this kind of stuff in public.

I've got to admit, I can relate to Josh. A few years ago, most of my friends and colleagues had no idea I was a Christian, even though my faith was important to me. But once after hearing the remarks at a relative's funeral, I wondered how people would remember me when I pass on. Would they merely remember a devoted Saints fan? A successful business owner? Maybe a guy who plays the piano at parties? This possibility bothered me. I resolved to become more vocal in expressing my faith.

VOCAL FANS, QUIET BELIEVERS

Please don't misunderstand. I'm not encouraging Christians to force their views on uninterested people. Such tactics are usually counterproductive. Nor am I advocating annoying behavior or obnoxiously wearing religion on one's sleeve. Are there any football teams you despise because of an obnoxious fan you know? It's the same thing.

Personally, I don't wear "Jesus is Cool" t-shirts, quote Bible verses during football games, or incessantly bring up God with my neighbors. I'm not saying these acts are wrong, but they just aren't my style. At the same time, silence isn't a good option. In Luke 8:38, Jesus tells a group of men to "return home and tell how much God has done for you." Shouldn't we want to do the same thing?

Talking about faith is easier than many people believe. If somebody asks about your weekend, simply mention you attended church before describing the Mexican restaurant you dined at. Consider placing a religious book on your desk at work—or your car seat. When eating lunch with colleagues or friends, mention that you're thinking about attending an interesting-sounding Bible study, but you have reservations. What do they think? Any of these non-intrusive acts can easily lead to conversations about faith. You might be surprised at how many people will respond to these invitations.

If you're bolder, tell somebody experiencing tough times you'll pray for her (or a loved one). Ask if it's all right to notify the prayer chain at your church (most people don't refuse prayers). And, yes, you can even pray together on the spot.

While you're at it, pass along this book to somebody who enjoys football. Better yet, form a group to discuss these topics. A full list of discussion questions can be found at www.faith360.org.

How about inviting a friend, relative or colleague to

church? Did you know it was Andrew that invited Simon Peter to meet Jesus? Andrew didn't offer clever arguments, quote Scriptures, or try to change Peter's bad habits. He simply invited Peter and allowed God to handle the rest (John 1:40-42). Imagine if Andrew had kept quiet or felt awkward about raising the subject. What if he assumed Peter wasn't interested? Perhaps Peter would have labored as a lowly fisherman throughout his entire life. Instead, Jesus transformed Peter and he became "the rock" on which Christ built his church (Matthew 16:18).

If you're already comfortable speaking about your faith, good for you! Your challenge is different. It may be a good time to reevaluate your witnessing efforts to make sure they're effective. The sad reality is that many folks (including Christians) are turned off by the comments of believers. Some enthusiastic people lay it on so thick that the words fall upon deaf ears. Others spout empty-sounding clichés or talk in jargon.

If you're excited about sharing your faith, do it in a way that produces maximum impact. Don't be a chatterbox. Listen. Show empathy. Think wisely. Effective communication is a two-way street. Your witnessing will become more powerful.

In short, look for ways to share your faith that make sense for your personality and environment. If you're entering uncharted waters, it's okay to feel apprehension. But as you try some of the easy-to-do ideas mentioned in this chapter, your concerns are likely to dissipate. And you know what? I have the sneaky suspicion God will raise your comfort meter to a higher level!

VOCAL FANS, QUIET BELIEVERS

PERSONAL JOURNAL

Write down any key points you want to remember:

_____
_____
_____
_____
_____

IMPORTANT VERSES

"Always be prepared to give an answer to everyone who asks you to give the reason for the hope that you have. But do this with gentleness and respect" (1 Peter 3:15).

"You are the light of the world. A city on a hill cannot be hidden. Neither do people light a lamp and put it under a bowl. Instead they put it on its stand, and it gives light to everyone in the house. In the same way, let your light shine before men, that they may see your good deeds and praise your Father in heaven" (Matthew 5:14-16).

"Not to us, O LORD, not to us but to your name be the glory, because of your love and faithfulness" (Psalm 115:1).

EXTRA "FILM" STUDY

Read Luke 8:26-39. Do Jesus' words apply to your life? How so?

WEEK 20
MOVING THE CHAINS

At all levels of football, one can find complacent and unmotivated players. Maybe they have reached previously set goals. Perhaps they landed a lucrative contract. Perhaps the problem is overconfidence, causing the athletes to believe they can coast and still enjoy success. Maybe they just don't want to be there.

Whatever the reason, such players no longer do what it takes to become better. They don't train diligently in the off season. Don't take care of their bodies. Don't pay attention in team meetings. In short, these athletes are not committed to taking their performance to the next level. Not interested in raising the bar.

A coach's job is, of course, to motivate players to reach their potential and contribute to the team's success. When confronted with a serious problem, a coach must often issue a wake-up call. Perhaps he "calls out" the player in front of his teammates or the media (remember when Bill Parcells referred to Terry Glenn as "she"?) Maybe the front office brings in a star free agent to challenge the complacent player for a starting position. Perhaps the coach benches the player or even places him on the *inactive* list. The objective is always the same: How can we get through to this player?

In the Gospels, Jesus encounters a similar situation when he meets a man complacent about his spiritual development. In Luke 18:18-23, the "rich young ruler" informs the Lord that he has followed all of God's commandments since he was a boy. Sounds a little cocky, huh?

Perhaps the confident ruler expected Jesus to give a high-five or say "well done." Instead, the Lord dropped a bombshell. "Sell everything you have and give to the poor. Then come, follow me." Uh-oh! At this the man's face fell, Luke writes. He went away sad, because he had great wealth. Talk about bursting this guy's bubble. Jesus had just issued a major wake-up call.

Like the rich young ruler, many Christians believe they are "good" people and are satisfied with their spiritual development. They are content. Comfortable. Not interested in raising the bar.

These folks may attend church on a regular basis—or they may not. They may do generous things for other people or participate in good causes—or they may not. These folks rarely claim they're perfect, but they aren't that concerned with their shortcomings. They are fine with the status quo. Do you know any Christians who fall into this category? In a survey of over one million churchgoers, researchers found that "half of all worshippers say they are not growing in their faith."[37]

It's difficult to understand such complacency after reading the Bible. Take the Sermon on the Mount, for instance. In Matthew 5, Jesus says to "give to the one who asks you" (v. 42), "love your enemies" (v. 44), and "turn ...the other [cheek]" (v. 39). He says that "anyone who looks at a woman lustfully has already committed adultery with her in his heart"(v. 28).

Unfortunately, many folks consider these commands as unrealistic and quickly disregard God's Word. But they are missing the point. By setting such lofty standards for behavior and conduct, Jesus challenges us to think differently about situations and relationships. He knows human beings tend to place limits on love and kindness, and He doesn't want to encourage that. He wants us to become more like Him. This means continuously raising the bar. When we take all of His commands seriously, we'll begin acting in ways we normally wouldn't consider, ways contrary to our selfish human nature.

When a coach "calls out" a player, the athlete can respond in different ways. He can deny the charges, stick his head in the sand, and be consumed with bitterness or anger. Alternatively, he can respond positively to constructive criticism and realize the coach has his best interests at heart. He then recommits himself to becoming the best player he can be. Down the road, he's usually thankful for the coach that pushed him to new heights.

In the same way, I'm thankful Jesus didn't give us a watered down, easy-to-implement plan for our lives. Can you imagine Jesus saying, "Lust is okay as long as you don't do it too much. Let's see, how about limiting pornography to only 15 minutes each day. Does that sound fair?" I'd say it sounds ridiculous, doesn't it?

If the Lord allows us to follow an easy road, we are shortchanged. Let's be thankful Jesus challenges us in ways that are difficult and sometimes uncomfortable. At the same time, we should be grateful the Lord loves us and forgives our many shortcomings.

So, let's recommit ourselves to the pursuit of knowing God and becoming more like Christ. Avoid self-righteousness and spiritual complacency. Study the Bible. Serve others. Pray frequently. Strive to live a holy life. Trust in God always.

BETWEEN THE TACKLES

Our goal isn't to obtain a ticket to heaven. Christ's sacrifice on the cross took care of that. The goal is to please the God we love and make an impact in our world. Progress may be slow—we may even lose yardage or turn the ball over. But our patient God gives us so many chances. Our goal, with God's help, should be to keep growing closer to the Lord. Keep learning to love our neighbors. Keep advancing. Keep *Moving the Chains*.

PERSONAL JOURNAL

Write down any key points you want to remember:

_____

_____

_____

_____

_____

IMPORTANT VERSES

"Be perfect, therefore, as your heavenly Father is perfect" (Matthew 5:48).

"But grow in the grace and knowledge of our Lord and Savior Jesus Christ" (2 Peter 3:18).

"Aim for perfection, listen to my appeal, be of one mind, live in peace" (2 Corinthians 13:11).

"We instructed you how to live in order to please God, as in fact you are living. Now we ask you and urge you in the Lord Jesus to do this more and more" (1 Thessalonians 4:1).

MOVING THE CHAINS

Extra "Film" Study

Read Matthew 5-8.

EPILOGUE
LEAVING IT ALL ON THE FIELD

The trip to Hawaii is like a mini-vacation. Pro-Bowl players enjoy "fun in the sun" before representing their teams in a nationally televised, all-star game. It's a great reward after a long, grueling season.

For fans watching on television, the experience is different. Not only is the outcome meaningless, it's the last game of the season. Die-hard fans must contemplate "life after football." There won't be meaningful games to watch for a *looong* time.

In reality, the season never ends for NFL teams. In his book *Patriot Reign*, Michael Holley described the conclusion of the 2002 season for the New England Patriots. On December 29, the defending Super Bowl champions played their final game of the regular season against the Miami Dolphins. The following morning, the 2002 squad met for the last time.

Holley writes, "How long does it take to switch one's focus from one season to the next? How about one shift? The squad meeting was at nine o'clock. At four o'clock, there was a 'needs meeting' in (Bill) Belichick's office. The coach, Ernie Adams, and Scott Pioli were all there with independent lists. They were charged with taking the first steps toward reconstructing the Patriots."[38] A new season had begun.

The Patriots aren't alone. All teams spend the "off-season" working diligently to upgrade their teams. Objectively assessing the results of the prior season. Setting off-season goals. Where must the team get better? What must be accomplished in the upcoming months?

In a similar manner, it's healthy to periodically evaluate our Christian journeys and even set goals. Where do you hope to make progress? What changes are you willing to make in your life? How can you become more like Christ? What steps can be taken to deepen your love for God and neighbor?

Like a team attempting to win a championship, we need to figure out *how* to move closer to achieving our objectives. Prayer is always a critical ingredient in this process, but specific action steps can also be helpful. Good intentions aren't enough. Sometimes we need a plan.

What should be in your plan? I encourage you to flip back through this book, taking note of items you underlined or highlighted. If you completed the "Personal Journal" after each chapter, review your notes. Determine which items require action. Make a commitment to follow through. Be intentional about your faith journey.

In 1 Corinthians 9:24-26, Paul uses a sports analogy to urge believers to fully devote themselves to knowing and serving Christ. He writes:

> "Do you not know that in a race all the runners run, but only one gets the prize? Run in such a way as to get the prize. Everyone who competes in the games goes into strict training. They do it to get a crown that will not last; but we do it to get a crown that will last forever."

LEAVING IT ALL ON THE FIELD

As described earlier, the Isthmian games were held near Corinth on a biennial basis. Competition was intense with athletes undergoing grueling training for months before the events. Not only did the training focus on strength, speed, endurance, technique, etc., it required the abandonment of freedoms or pleasures that stood in the way of success. Like today, committed athletes made great sacrifices with hopes of winning the "prize."

When Paul encourages believers to "run in such a way as to get the prize," he urges us to make a similar commitment to Jesus Christ. Give 110 percent. Don't hold back. Put it all on the line. If athletes are willing to display such devotion to obtain perishable prizes, Christians have a far greater reason to be committed.

Final Thought

In week 13 of the 2006 NFL season, rookie Reggie Bush enjoyed his "break-out" game by scoring four touchdowns against the San Francisco 49ers. His high school coach, Gordon Woods, attended the game and was asked about coaching Bush. He replied:

> "Well, I'll never forget that last game Reggie played for me. He was sensational. But we came up short. Talk about leaving it all out on the field. He could hardly move. Completely exhausted. He's in the locker room, and he's getting the IV treatments. We wanted him to stay overnight and just rest. But he kept insisting on getting on the bus with the team for the trip back home. Of all the great things he did for the school, that's how I'll remember Reggie. The gladiator warrior who always paid the price."[39]

How will you be remembered? Are you prepared to leave everything on the field? Will you give it your best shot? Are you ready to throw yourself into the cause of the gracious God who made your salvation possible? Will you go the extra mile to love neighbors and even strangers? What will be your legacy? Are you a warrior?

Make no mistake about it. You have an opportunity to make a tremendous difference on Earth. Pray you will follow as God leads you in the right direction. With God's help, perhaps some day you'll be able to confidently proclaim the same words as Paul,

> "I have fought the good fight, I have finished the race, I have kept the faith. Now there is in store for me the crown of righteousness, which the Lord, the righteous Judge, will award to me on that day" (2 Timothy 4:7-8).

APPENDIX
FORMING A DISCUSSION GROUP

If you found this book useful, consider forming a discussion group with other football fans. When Christians engage in dialogue with other believers and seekers, it can be a learning experience and fellowship opportunity. Because of this book's subject matter, it may provide an excellent opportunity to have conversations with believers who typically shy away from standard religious books or curriculum.

WHAT WILL YOU TALK ABOUT?

Like a traditional book club, you can always meet to discuss an assigned chapter. No agenda. Just show up and talk. Alternatively, use discussion questions to facilitate conversations. At www.movingthechains.net, I have provided questions for each chapter in this book. Feel free to add or delete from the list.

WHERE SHOULD YOUR GROUP MEET?

Your group can meet anywhere. Perhaps you'll want to invite friends or neighbors to your home. Maybe you can form a discussion group with colleagues at work. Meet before or after work hours or even during lunch.

Another option is to form a "small group" at your church. This can be an effective way to get to know people in your congregation. At my church, a "Monday Night Football" group meets throughout football season. The men and women hold a short Bible study before watching the first half of the game together. You can use this same approach in your home.

DISCUSSION TIPS

In today's world, a tremendous amount of dialogue occurs at a superficial level while "real" or important topics are avoided or brushed over. The group leader's goal should be to prevent this from happening. Provide a safe and encouraging atmosphere so members feel comfortable in opening up and sharing honest thoughts. You may also want to encourage or challenge all members to examine the subjects with open minds. It won't be surprising if some individuals tend to be stuck in their ways and beliefs.

Keep alert for ways to put ideas and knowledge into action. Author Josh Hunt wrote, "Our job in Christian education is not to make smarter sinners. Our job is to make disciples."[40] Learning about the Bible (or other faith-related topics) can be fascinating, but this is not the ultimate goal. The objective is to help people become more committed disciples of Jesus Christ.

Along these lines, some individuals might be interested in utilizing other members to promote accountability. Perhaps they can "report back" to the group on whether they've applied certain ideas in their lives. Alternatively, a person can select another individual in the group to communicate with on a frequent basis about spiritual matters and growth.

FORMING A DISCUSSION GROUP

IMPROVING YOUR FACILITATION SKILLS

As mentioned, your goal is to facilitate open and honest conversation. Here are some general tips to enhance your facilitation skills. This advice is not "rocket science"; however, many group leaders fail to implement these ideas because they require discipline.

Maximize Group Involvement. Attempt to include everyone in the discussion. Without guidance from a facilitator, certain participants often dominate conversations while others remain in silence. While equal contributions are not always necessary (or even desirable), your job is to ensure that contributions are appropriately balanced.

To encourage participation from a quiet individual (or to stifle a talkative person), consider these techniques:
- call on individuals directly (just be careful not to embarrass anybody);
- ask a quiet person to read a Biblical passage (or other reading);
- break into smaller discussion groups; and
- conduct surveys or implement other ways that allow everyone to participate.

Make Members Feel Comfortable. To achieve maximum participation, it's essential that participants feel comfortable. This is particularly important when visitors or new people join a group. One of the biggest reasons why people fail to speak up is the fear of saying something "stupid." The leader can do several things to mitigate such feelings, including acknowledging all opinions, never demeaning or ignoring comments, referring to a new person's comments later in the meeting (thus showing they were heard), etc. In addition, the leader can ask easy questions to get people comfortable in participating.

Manage the Agenda and Group Dynamics. In a group setting, it's easy to get off track from the planned agenda. Therefore, the leader has an important role to play in ensuring that meetings are productive. If an individual takes the group off point, don't be afraid to "rein the group back in."

USEFUL RESOURCES

A variety of information on "small groups" can be found on the Internet. I've also found the following books to be helpful:

Leading Life-Changing Small Groups, Bill Donahue (Zondervan)

You Can Double Your Class in Two Years or Less, Josh Hunt (Group Publishing)

The Seven Deadly Sins of Small Group Ministry, Bill Donahue and Russ Robinson (Zondervan)

ENDNOTES

1 Electronic Arts (EA) press release, *EA's MADDEN NFL 07 Returns Opening Week Kick-Off With Biggest Retail Performance Ever*, August 31, 2006.

2 "Electric Football" was a top-selling board game in the United States during the 1960s and 1970s. Sales slumped in the 1980s, but the game has once again become popular. For more information, visit www.miggle.com.

3 This is a reference to Joe Namath's conversation with ESPN's sideline reporter Suzy Kolber during the Patriots-Jets game on December 20, 2003. During the interview, Namath repeatedly told Kolber that he wanted to kiss her!

4 C.S. Lewis, *Mere Christianity* (San Francisco, CA, Harper SanFrancisco, 1952), p. 142.

5 Josh Hunt, *You Can Double Your Class in Two Years or Less* (Loveland, CO, Group Publishing, 1997), p. 27.

6 William L. Holladay, *Long Ago God Spoke* (Minneapolis, MN, Fortress Press, 1995), p. 65.

7 John Feinstein, *Next Man Up* (New York, NY, Little, Brown and Company, 2005), p. 179.

8 C.S. Lewis, *Mere Christianity*, p. 210-211.

[9] Jerry B. Jenkins, *Writing for the Soul* (Cincinnati, OH, Writer's Digest Books, 2006), p. 64-65.

[10] Kerry Dearborn, *Love at the Heart of the Universe*, Christian History & Biography, Issue 86, Spring 2005, p. 34.

[11] These statistics were obtained from www.warrickdunnfoundation.org as of August 2007.

[12] Peter King, *Dunn Appeals to NFL Players*, www.si.com, September 1, 2005.

[13] Sam Farmer, *Caring to Share*, LA Times; September 1, 2006.

[14] Kenneth C. Haugk, *Don't Sing Songs to a Heavy Heart* (St. Louis, MI, Stephen Ministries, 2004).

[15] For more information on Stephen Ministers, visit www.stephenministries.org.

[16] The height and weight of Jonathan Ogden and Martin Gramatica were obtained from the official web sites of the Baltimore Ravens and Dallas Cowboys, respectively, during the 2006 season.

[17] Michael Lewis, *The Blind Side* (New York, NY, W.W. Norton & Company, 2006), p. 95.

[18] George Barna, *Revolution* (Carol Stream, IL, Tyndale House Publishers, 2005), p. 31-32.

[19] Article at www.sportsillustrated.cnn.com, *Saints Celebrate*; April 17, 1999

[20] The quote was obtained from www.wikipedia.org.

[21] Os Hillman, *Faith@Work: What Every Pastor and Church Leader Should Know* (Cumming, GA, Aslan Group Publishing, 2004), p. 127.

[22] Mel Graham, "Being Bold for Christ," *Decision* (Charlotte, NC, Billy Graham Evangelistic Association, July-August 2004), p. 35.

[23] John C. Maxwell, *Life@Work Handbook* (Nashville, TN, Nelson Impact, 2005), p. 81.

[24] Harold Myra, *A Greater Vision*, Christianity Today, October 2006, p. 90.

[25] "Readings in World Christian History, Vol. I: Earliest Christianity to 1453" (Maryknoll, NY, Orbis Books, 2004), p. 15.

ENDNOTES

[26] John C. Maxwell, *Life@Work Handbook*, p. 81.

[27] David P. Gushee, *How to Create Cynics*, Christianity Today, September 2006, p. 114.

[28] This is one of the most well-known quotes of J.C. Watts Jr.

[29] Athanasius, *The King Visits Earth*, Christian History & Biography, Issue 51, Vol. XV, No. 3, (Carol Stream, IL, Christianity Today, 1996), p. 16.

[30] John Corrigan, Frederick M. Denny, Carlos M.N. Eire and Martin S. Jaffee, *Jews, Christians, Muslims: A Comparative Introduction to Monotheistic Religions* (Upper Saddle River, NJ, Prentice Hall, 1998), p. 115.

[31] John Corrigan, Frederick M. Denny, Carlos M.N. Eire and Martin S. Jaffee, *Jews, Christians, Muslims: A Comparative Introduction to Monotheistic Religions*, p. 115.

[32] Bruce L. Shelley, *Church History in Plain Language* (Nashville, TN, Thomas Nelson Publishers, 1995), p. 3.

[33] Joe Gibbs, *Racing to Win* (Colorado Springs, CO, Multnomah Publishers Inc., 2002), p. 276.

[34] The web addresses for these organizations are www.bsfinternational.org and www.communitybiblestudy.org, respectively.

[35] Spiritual Classics, *Christianity Today*, September 2006, Vol. 50, No. 9 (Carol Stream, IL, Christianity Today, 2006), p. 112.

[36] Drew Brees, a statement made on August 31, 2006 after the Saints' final preseason game.

[37] Cynthia Woolever and Deborah Bruce, *A Field Guide to U.S. Congregations* (Louisville, KN, Westminster John Knox Press, 2002), p. 35.

[38] Michael Holley, *Patriot Reign* (New York, NY, HarperCollins Publishers, 2004), p. 132.

[39] Peter Finney, *Relaxed Bush Breaks Loose*, Times-Picayune, December 4, 2006.

[40] Josh Hunt, *You Can Double Your Class in Two Years or Less*, p. 26.

INDEX OF BIBLICAL REFERENCES

Old Testament

Genesis 1:27	110
Genesis 3:12	46
Genesis 4:1-10	48
Genesis 4:9	47
Genesis 11:1-9	25
Genesis 12:2	25
Genesis 13:1-11	82
Genesis 13:8-9	80
Genesis 15-16	99
Genesis 25	79
Genesis 25:29-34	82
Genesis 25:31	80
Genesis 39	103
Exodus 3:6	30
Exodus 19:16-19	32
Exodus 20:18-20	29
Exodus 32:1-24	46

Reference	Page
Leviticus 19:9-10	56
Deuteronomy 6:5	28
Deuteronomy 6:6-7	117
Deuteronomy 6:13	28
Deuteronomy 15:11	56
Judges 15	37
1 Samuel 1:10-16	18
1 Samuel 13:7-14	24
1 Samuel 15	24
1 Samuel 16:7	21
1 Samuel 17	76
1 Samuel 17:10	73
1 Samuel 17:38-40	74
1 Samuel 25	35
2 Samuel 11:2-5	46-47
2 Samuel 12:13	47
2 Samuel 16	34
2 Samuel 16:13-14	35
1 Chronicles 29	58, 59
Job 38-39	32
Psalm 18:27	26
Psalm 19:7-8,10	69
Psalm 22:2	99
Psalm 51	47, 48
Psalm 86:5	48
Psalm 103:11	31
Psalm 115:1	123
Psalm 119	71
Psalm 119:105	114
Psalm 119:48	71
Psalm 119:89	117
Psalm 139	105

BIBLICAL REFERENCES

Psalm 139:1-4 103
Psalm 145:8-9 111
Proverbs 1:7 31
Proverbs 3:9 61
Proverbs 3:28 59
Proverbs 4:14-15 93
Proverbs 11:25 59
Proverbs 15:1 36
Proverbs 12:16 36
Proverbs 15:3 102
Proverbs 22:1 82
Proverbs 27:21 25
Isaiah 6:1-5 32
Isaiah 6:5 30
Isaiah 53 111
Isaiah 55:8 99
Isaiah 40:11 31
Ezekiel 1:25-28 32
Daniel 1 88

New Testament

Matthew 5-8 129
Matthew 5:14-16 123
Matthew 5:28 126
Matthew 5:29-30 .... 91, 93
Matthew 5:39 126
Matthew 5:42 126
Matthew 5:44 126
Matthew 5:48 128
Matthew 7:1 19
Matthew 7:3 19

Reference	Page
Matthew 15:12-16	114
Matthew 16:18	122
Matthew 17:1-8	30, 32
Matthew 19:26	42
Matthew 22:36-40	15
Matthew 25:14-30	84, 88
Matthew 25:31-46	63, 65
Mark 1:21-37	117
Mark 4:13	114
Mark 8:21	114
Mark 12:41-44	58
Luke 6:46-49	117
Luke 8:38	121
Luke 8:26-39	123
Luke 12:13-34	59
Luke 14:11	26
Luke 14:12-14	64
Luke 18:1-7	105
Luke 18:9-14	21
Luke 18:18-23	126
Luke 23:39-43	53
John 1:40-42	122
John 3:16	53
John 8:1-11	21
John 8:54	120
John 10:10	41
John 13:1-17	26
John 14:15	42
John 15:13	110
Acts 14:8-18	26
Acts 16:31	53
Romans 2:1-2	19

BIBLICAL REFERENCES

Romans 3:22 70
Romans 3:23 68
Romans 6:23 68
Romans 7 67
Romans 7:7 69
Romans 7:15 41
Romans 8:11 104
Romans 8:17 110
Romans 8:38-39 43
Romans 10:9 53
Romans 12:18 82
Romans 14:4 21
Romans 14:13 21
1 Corinthians 2:9 51
1 Corinthians 9:24 11
1 Corinthians 9:24-26 132
1 Corinthians 10:13 ....93, 105
1 Corinthians 12:4-6 87
1 Corinthians 13:4-8 43
2 Corinthians 3:3 87
2 Corinthians 5:20 87
2 Corinthians 8:1-4 58
2 Corinthians 8:9 111
2 Corinthians 9:7 59
2 Corinthians 13:11 128
Galatians 2:16 51
Galatians 3 71
Galatians 3:10 68
Galatians 3:24 71
Galatians 5:14 71
Galatians 5:22-23 37
Galatians 6:9-10 64

Ephesians 2:8	51
Ephesians 3:18-19	110
Ephesians 6:11-12	96
Philippians 2:3	26
Philippians 4:13	42, 105
Colossians 3:12-15	37
Colossians 3:17	87
Colossians 3:23-24	85
1 Thessalonians 4:1	128
1 Thessalonians 5:11	21
1 Thessalonians 5:15	36
1 Timothy 1:12-17	43
1 Timothy 1:15	42
1 Timothy 6:17-18	57
2 Timothy 3:16-17	117
2 Timothy 4:7-8	134
Hebrews 4:12	117
Hebrews 4:13	105
Hebrews 9:28	41
Hebrews 12:14	82
James 2:17	52
James 4:7	93
James 4:8	76, 116
1 Peter 1:15	102
1 Peter 2:9	84
1 Peter 2:17	26
1 Peter 3:9	37
1 Peter 3:15	123
2 Peter 3:9	110
2 Peter 3:18	128
1 John 1:8-9	48
1 John 1:9	41

BIBLICAL REFERENCES

1 John 3:16 111
1 John 3:17-18 56
1 John 4:8 . . . . .43, 110
1 John 4:9 111

INDEX OF FOOTBALL PLAYERS, COACHES AND COMMENTATORS

Adams, Ernie 131
Alexander, Shaun 77
Anderson, Gary 34
Bailey, Champ 57
Belichick, Bill 131
Bosworth, Brian 88
Brees, Drew 116
Brooks, Aaron 45
Brown, Orlando 33
Bush, Reggie 55-56, 133
Coughlin, Tom 28
Cowher, Bill 27, 32
Ditka, Mike 79-80
Dugny, Tony 86
Dunn, Warrick 55
Faulk, Marshall 77
Favre, Brett 91, 93
Fischer, Jeff 32
Gannon, Rich 40

151

Gibbs, Joe 86, 114
Glenn, Terry 125
Gramatica, Martin 73
Gruden, Jon 113, 114
Haynesworth, Albert 101
Johnson, Chad 17, 18
Kearse, Javon 34
Kolber, Suzy 14
Leaf, Ryan 83, 88
Lewis, Ray 13-14, 29
Lynch, John 57
Mandarich, Tony 88
Manning, Eli 18
Manning, Peyton 13, 40
Marino, Dan 40
McNabb, Donavan 24, 77
Namath, Joe 15
Ogden, Jonathan 73
Owens, Terrell 23-24
Palmer, Carson 17
Parcells, Bill 125
Phillips, Lawrence 88
Pioli, Scott 131
Rice, Jerry 24, 107-108
Rogers, Charles 83
Saunders, Al 113
Simms, Chris 113
Smith, Akili 82, 88
Testaverde, Vinny 40, 43
Turner, Norv 27
Vick, Michael 77
Walsh, Bill 74

FOOTBALL PLAYERS, COACHES AND COMMENTATORS

Ward, Hines 61
Warner, Kurt 86
Watts, J.C. 102
Williams, Ricky 79-80, 82
Woods, Gordon 133
Young, Steve 23-24
Young, Vince 14

INDEX OF FOOTBALL TEAMS

NFL Teams

Arizona Cardinals 86
Atlanta Falcons 55
Baltimore Ravens 28, 33-34, 43, 73
Chicago Bears 119-120
Cincinnati Bengals 17, 82
Cleveland Browns 43, 119
Dallas Cowboys 23-24
Denver Broncos 57
Detroit Lions 83
Green Bay Packers 119
Indianapolis Colts 40
Miami Dolphins 119, 131
Minnesota Vikings 55, 119
New England Patriots 43, 74, 131-132
New Orleans Saints 12, 55, 79, 81, 82, 90-91, 113, 116
New York Giants 28
New York Jets 43

Oakland Raiders 119
Philadelphia Eagles 23, 24
Pittsburgh Steelers 27, 32, 61
San Diego Chargers 83
San Francisco 49ers 23, 24, 133
Tampa Bay Buccaneers 43, 113
Tennessee Titans 32, 34, 101
Washington Redskins 28, 79, 81-82, 86, 113

College Teams

Florida State 119
Miami 43
Michigan 14
Michigan State 88
Nebraska 88
Oklahoma 88, 102
Oregon 88
Penn State 12
Texas 79
USC 119
Washington State 83, 88

For more information about **BETWEEN THE TACKLES,** visit www.faith360.org.

At **www.faith360.org** you can:
- purchase additional copies of **BETWEEN THE TACKLES** (volume discounts are available)
- obtain a listing of discussion questions for group or individual study, and
- access Tom Houck's commentary on the book.

Faith360 also provides other content by Tom Houck such as videos, devotionals, and blogs to help you advance in your faith journey.